CRITICAL THINKING

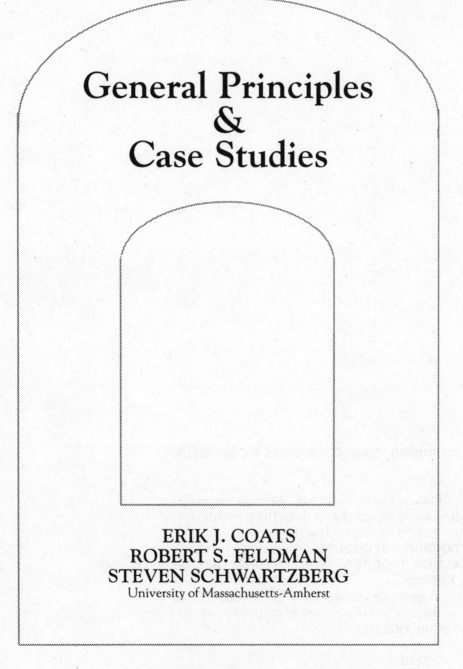

General Principles
&
Case Studies

ERIK J. COATS
ROBERT S. FELDMAN
STEVEN SCHWARTZBERG
University of Massachusetts-Amherst

McGraw-Hill, Inc.

New York St. Louis San Francisco Auckland Bogotá Caracas Lisbon
London Madrid Mexico City Milan Montreal New Delhi
San Juan Singapore Sydney Tokyo Toronto

Critical Thinking: General Principles and Case Studies

Erik J. Coats, Robert S. Feldman, and Steven Schwartzberg

University of Massachusetts at Amherst

I. General Principles

Part II: Case Studies

Critical Thinking: General Principles and Case Studies

Critical Thinking: General Principles and Case Studies

What's In It for You:
An Introduction to Critical Thinking

Maria smokes a pack of cigarettes a day. Concerned about her health, you would like her to quit. You tell her that doctors think smoking is a dangerous habit, but she answers that doctors have been wrong before, so why should she believe them...and furthermore, why should she believe you? Even after this rebuff, you are still concerned. How would you try to convince her to stop smoking?

Betty has just bought a new compact disc by her favorite artist, and she is eager to listen to it. She gets home, flips on the power switch of the stereo, and...nothing happens. She again turns the power button off and on, but still nothing happens. What should she do next?

Wade Boggs, a star player of the New York Yankees, performs an elaborate set of pre-game and mid-game rituals throughout the baseball season. According to one news report, "he eats specific foods on specific days, leaves for the ball park at the same time each day, takes the same number of practice grounders from the same coach, runs his sprints at the same time, runs to his position retracing his exact footprints, and draws the Hebrew symbol <u>chai</u> ("life") in the dirt each time he steps up to home plate" (Boston Globe Magazine, April 9, 1989, p. 44). Boggs believes that he needs to complete these exacting rituals in order to play the game successfully. How would you assess the logic of his claim?

What do these scenarios have in common? They all involve <u>critical thinking</u>. Whether evaluating a scientific research experiment or figuring out what might be wrong with a broken home appliance, critical thinking is an important and common tool of everyday life. Don't let the term frighten you; its applications are endless, it is a skill that can be practiced and honed, and it is extremely likely that you already do it, without realizing it, in many situations.

What characterizes critical thinking? People who think critically scrutinize the assumptions that underlie their decisions, beliefs, and actions. When presented with a new idea or a persuasive argument, they carefully evaluate it, checking for logical consistency and listening for tacit assumptions that may distort the central point. They pay attention to the context in which ideas or actions are implemented. Wary of "quick-fix" solutions and absolute claims, critical thinkers are skeptical of simple answers to complex questions. And rather than accepting pat, stock, or proverbial answers, critical thinkers attempt to develop alternate ways of understanding situations and taking action.

Although it may at first sound daunting, the consistent application of critical thinking can be learned quite readily. The reason is that ability to think critically is not something that a person is innately born with, and it is not equivalent to measurable intelligence. Instead, it is a <u>process</u> of thinking, in which a few basic principles can be applied to a vast array of situations. Like versatile tools with many uses, the principles of critical thinking can serve as a kind of cognitive tool-kit. With a little practice, you can use these guidelines flexibly and creatively to tackle everyday problems, clarify your own position on difficult social issues, evaluate scientific research, and become a more educated consumer of the information you hear and read.

Your understanding of the world probably already embodies some of these basic principles of critical thinking. For example, consider the situation faced by Betty, whose stereo is malfunctioning. What would be your next step?

After determining that the stereo <u>should</u> be working (and questioning basic assumptions such as this is often the first step of critical thinking), you would probably try to define the problem as precisely as possible. For example, you might first try to determine if the electricity is out by turning on a lamp or looking at an electric clock to make sure other electrical appliances are working. (If they are not, you would need to explore a new set of questions, focusing more on the situation than on the stereo: Is it a blown fuse? Is it just one room, or the whole apartment, or the entire street?).

Assuming that other appliances are working, you might then investigate if the electrical socket is defective. To do this, you might plug the functioning lamp into the stereo socket. If the lamp works, you might then plug the stereo into the socket where the lamp had been, and - if the stereo still doesn't work - you would now know that the electricity worked and the sockets worked, but the stereo does not.

Critical thinking, unfortunately, wouldn't be able to help you fix the complex circuitry inside the stereo, and it would have to be taken to a repair shop. But approaching the problem critically does play a vital role in identifying the source of the problem. By examining assumptions about whether the stereo should be working, and by logically and systematically exploring various possibilities of what might be wrong, the problem can be defined as precisely and appropriately as possible.

This simple example illustrates just one way of thinking critically in everyday life. As we will see, the same principles involved in diagnosing the stereo problem can also be applied to many other situations.

<u>Critical Thinking and Psychology</u>

Although the scope of critical thinking is broader than any one topic, the skills involved will come in handy in your introduction to the field of psychology.

For the beginning student, studying psychology often can seem to be an overwhelming task. A brief glance through any introductory psychology textbook indicates the enormous breadth of the field, ranging from the microscopic study of a nerve cell and the analysis of human social behavior in emergency situations to teaching language to chimpanzees and the theoretical rationales for psychotherapy.

Because of the nature of the field, psychology requires the consistent use of the principles of critical thinking. For one thing, psychology is a discipline that examines human phenomena at different <u>levels of analysis</u>. At times, psychologists attempt to answer questions that are <u>molecular</u> -- extremely specific and detailed. At other times, they must take a <u>molar</u> view, examining the "big picture" rather than isolated details. When studying psychology, then, the following questions, central in critical thinking, must always be asked: What is the level at which this topic is being discussed? How would the same topic look from a different level?

Furthermore, psychologists hold a unique vantage point on human nature (Winter, 1984). The psychological conception of humankind differs from the view of other disciplines -- for example, the economic view of people as rational actors, the legal view of a "reasonable or just person," or the theological view of humanity in the context of religion. Psychology offers a specific -- and unique -- perspective on human behavior. As you will learn, psychologists differ greatly in their theories regarding why humans function the way they do. At the same time, psychologists also share certain common beliefs. As you study the field, it is crucial that you are able to identify what those shared beliefs are, and challenge them to see if they fit with your experience.

Finally, psychology is a discipline committed to scientific research. Yet research -- in the field of psychology, in other sciences, and in the general culture -- can easily be misapplied, misinterpreted, or taken out of context. Critical thinking will help you evaluate the merits and dangers of scientific research. Some educators believe that learning to evaluate research critically is one of the most important skills that an introductory course in psychology can teach (e.g., Winter, 1984).

To aid your critical thinking skills, we will describe what critical thinking is, highlight the ways in which you already think critically, and point you in the right direction to further develop the requisite skills. Of course, learning to think critically won't happen without effort and practice; there are no easy solutions. (Remember: critical thinkers reject "quick-fix" solutions and are skeptical of simple answers to complex questions). While the concepts presented here should all be easy to understand, you need to experiment with them, to try them out on your own, and to apply them to different situations.

Before actually discussing the principles involved, however, an important question needs to be asked: Can critical thinking be taught at all? A brief look at changing ideas about education over the past 100 years can help provide an answer.

Some Background on Critical Thinking

Had you completed your secondary education in the mid to late 19th century, the philosophy guiding your schooling would have been fundamentally different than the one which is guiding your more contemporary education. While one of the primary goals of education -- teaching students to think critically -- has remained the same throughout, beliefs about how to accomplish this goal have changed dramatically.

Until the early 20th century, educators believed in the "formal discipline" of the mind. By studying certain fields, such as logic, grammar, and mathematics, it was felt that a person's intellect could be flexibly developed across a range of situations and disciplines. The idea was somewhat similar to the way one engages in physical exercise to gain muscular strength. Specific intellectual capacities, such as memorization, were treated analogously to muscles -- the more one exercised them, the theory went, the stronger they became (Nisbett, Fong, Lehman & Cheng, 1987).

For example, students were taught Latin because it is a complex language requiring a lot of memorization. Educators believed that this helped students' intellectual abilities in many different situations. Latin was not taught because of its everyday importance; it was taught so that the skills developed from learning it could be transferred to other intellectual pursuits.

Despite the appeal of the notion that the mind could be exercised to gain strength, like a muscle, psychologists in the early 1900s adamantly rejected this long-standing principle (James, 1899; Thorndike, 1906, 1913). They argued that intellectual abilities were highly task-specific and that skills did not transfer from one field of study to another. Largely through their influence, 20th century school curricula moved away from the idea of formal discipline, which had been the cornerstone of educational philosophy (Nisbett et al., 1987).

Recently, however, psychologists and educators have begun re-examining the potential value of learning specific cognitive strategies that can be broadly applied (e.g., Brookfield, 1987; D'Angelo, 1987; Halpern, 1984; Nisbett et al, 1987; Sternberg & Caruso, 1985; Stemberg & Wanger, 1986; Winter, 1984). Current research (e.g., Lehman, Lempert & Nisbett, 1988; Nisbett et al, 1987; Stemberg & Wanger, 1986) suggests that certain aspects of the formal discipline model deserve to be salvaged, and that some skills (such as using inductive reasoning and applying abstract logic to pragmatic situations) can transfer across situations.

While it is probably not the case, then, that learning Latin will make you more intelligent, there are benefits to learning abstract, general concepts that can transfer to different academic and practical tasks. In other words, the skills of critical thinking can be learned, and individuals can improve their abilities to think logically, coherently, and critically.

However, before considering these specific principles of critical thinking, we need to consider the ways in which people come to know the things they know.

KNOWING WHAT WE KNOW:
SOURCES OF OUR KNOWLEDGE

Obesity is bad for your health. The earth revolves around the sun. 6 x 5 = 30. A picture is worth a thousand words.

All of us know a great deal of information. Some of it has been learned formally, in school. Some we have learned through the media -- television, movies, newspapers. And for many other things, although we feel we "know" them, we're not sure where or how they were learned. How does a person come to believe that something is true?

Around the turn of the century, the American philosopher Charles Peirce theorized that there are at least four ways in which individuals come to "know" something (Peirce, 1960). He labeled these four means of knowing as the method of tenacity, the method of authority, the a priori method, and the scientific method.

Method of Tenacity. According to the method of tenacity, a person believes certain ideas to be true primarily because those ideas have been around for a long time. Rather than questioning an idea's validity or testing its merit, the idea is accepted because of its longevity -- if it has survived so long, it must be true.

From the vantage point of critical thinking, tenacity is a poor method to determine if something is true. Simply because a person has always believed something is not, by itself, a reason to continue believing it. (People continued to believe that the sun revolved around the earth long after Copernicus proved that the reverse was true). Yet why do people cling to old beliefs?

One reason may be that our cognitive systems are actually biased towards remembering and preferring information that we already know. Psychologists use the word schema to mean the organized and stored knowledge that a person holds on a given topic. Each of us has many cognitive schemas, ranging from what we may know about football and how much we like certain foods to perceptions of our own physical appearance. Research on schemas indicates that they are very resistant to change (for a review see Fiske & Taylor, 1984). Because of schemas, we encode new information in a framework that is strongly influenced by what we already know. Old ideas then, aren't discarded easily, and people have a tendency to continue to believe what they've always believed.

Method of Authority. A second way of knowing something is the method of authority. People judge certain information to be true because it comes from a source of authority -- a scientist, the government, a parent, a teacher, an expert of some sort. Advertisers easily take advantage of the method of authority to help sell their products; how much more likely we are to buy something that "leading experts" use, "four out of five doctors recommend," or "scientists have proven" to be superior to the competition!

While you may be thinking, "I'm too smart for that -- I'm not going to believe something just because someone in authority tells me it's so," the method of authority is actually much more influential in our lives than you might at first acknowledge. As an example, think for a moment about something you most likely take for granted: that cigarette smoking is unhealthy. Ask yourself why you believe that it is unhealthy. If you answered "because it causes cancer and other diseases," then ask yourself how you know that it causes diseases. Most likely, the answer is that scientists, the United States Surgeon General, and maybe teachers and your parents have told you it is unhealthy. In other words, you believe cigarettes are unhealthy because voices of authority have said that it is so.

In fact, cigarette smoking is related to many adverse health effects, and physicians have accrued overwhelming evidence which links cigarettes with a variety of diseases. But you shouldn't rely on their word for it. As a critical thinker, you need to draw an important distinction: cigarette smoking is not unhealthy because medical experts say it is unhealthy. Instead, it is unhealthy because scientific data have been gathered to implicate it in life-threatening illnesses. To determine for yourself whether smoking is unhealthy, then, you may want to read the actual scientific reports, or at least summaries of the reports, on the subject.

As with the method of tenacity, critical thinkers regard the method of authority as an unsatisfactory means of determining if something is true. Of course, what an expert in a certain field tells us may very well be true, but it is not going to be true simply because of the person's stature. In fact, here is what a medical guidebook for pregnant women had to say about cigarette smoking in 1957 -- advice that sounds startling to modern ears:

> By no means try to give up [cigarette smoking] in
> pregnancy. There is no surer way of upsetting the
> nerves at a period when you should be calm...even the
> most inveterate smoker can usually be content with a
> package a day or somewhat less, and if you arrange
> this there is no great cause for concern (Eastman, 1957,
> p. 78).

A Priori Method. Whereas the methods of tenacity and authority do not rely on critical thinking, the a priori method employs rudimentary skills of logic and deduction in determining if something is true. With this method, a person hypothesizes that a cause and effect relationship exists between two variables, or speculates about a general rule based on a particular incident. Something is deemed to be true based on informal and uncontrolled observation.

For example, Maria worked as a sales assistant in a gardening store. She was in a particularly good mood one day, and smiled a great deal. At the day's end, she realized that she had sold more merchandise that day than ever before, and she decided that the customers had bought more because she had been smiling. She further decided that salesclerks should always smile.

Maria is reasoning from the a priori method. She has taken a specific event -- her smiling at customers -- and decided that this caused the increase in sales. It might have...but can she be sure? Perhaps that day would have been a record sales day anyway, whether or not she was smiling. Or, perhaps Maria was doing something in addition to smiling that helped sales, such as flattering the customers. In other words, Maria is basing her decision on uncontrolled observation, and although she may be right, it also may be that her smiling was irrelevant.

Maria also believed that her smiling (a particular incident) would increase sales for all salespeople (a general rule). This, again, is an example of a priori reasoning.

The a priori method is more sophisticated and involves more critical thinking than the methods of tenacity or authority. This is because it relies on observation and the forming of hypotheses. But it still lacks the rigor and control of the scientific method (discussed next). Because it is done informally, without any way to check or verify the information, it can easily lead to wrong conclusions. Reasoning by the a priori method is at the heart of many superstitious beliefs. And sometimes, it can lead to "logical" conclusions that are silly or absurd.

For example, let's return to the case of Wade Boggs. He believes that the elaborate rituals he performs daily throughout the baseball season make him a better ballplayer. While he is unquestioningly a superb hitter, it may be that he's only batting average when it comes to critical thinking. Boggs is reasoning from the a priori method; he has informally observed two events and concluded that a causal relationship exists between them. He believes that Variable A (his ritualized routines) cause Variable B (his success at the game). While his superstitious actions have likely become habitual, his deduction that they cause his success is probably false. Only the scientific method can accurately determine if this is the case.

Scientific Method. The scientific method relies on critical thinking and is the soundest means of determining if something is true. It involves controlled experimentation and reaching conclusions that are rational and supported by evidence. But don't get the idea that the scientific method is something limited to crusty, humorless scientists tediously working in some antiseptic laboratory. It is a way of knowing or determining something to be true that has everyday applications.

Let's go back to Maria's conclusion that because she smiled, she sold more merchandise. She wondered if this belief was accurate or not, and so in order to find out, she designed a little experiment.

Maria conducted her experiment at the store. Because she knew that the busiest shopping hours were between 2:00 and 4:00 every afternoon, she selected that time for her study. She decided that on alternating days during those hours, she would either continually smile, or not smile at all. Except for changing her smile, she attempted to present herself the same way in all other regards. At first, she thought she might only do this for two afternoons, but then realized that this would not be enough time to establish a consistent trend. So she conducted her experiment for two weeks, at the end of which she compared her total sales for the two hour block on the smiling and non-smiling days.

Let's say that Maria's total sales were significantly higher for the smiling days than for the non-smiling days. Assuming that she had kept everything else the same, and had systematically alternated the days when she was or wasn't smiling, she would be in a much stronger position to claim that her smiling had led to increased sales than before.

Now imagine a slightly different scenario. Let's say that Maria had not been purposely changing her smile in a systematic way. However, at the end of each work day, she noted in her diary whether or not she had been smiling. After two weeks, she read her diary, and discovered that on days she had been smiling, she sold more merchandise. In this case, could she determine that her smiling caused the increased sales?

No. If this were all the information Maria had, she might be able to determine that smiling and increased sales were related to one another, but she could not say which caused which. Her smiling might have led to increased sales, but it is also possible that good sales days caused her to smile more.

Frequently, two events that are correlated are interpreted as having a cause and effect relationship. However, <u>correlation is not the same as causality.</u> Determining that one event has caused another is more difficult than determining that they are related.

What is needed to determine cause and effect between two variables? According to the philosopher John Stuart Mill, three conditions must ideally be met to determine causality. Without them, the cause and effect of two variables (here labelled A and B) can be guessed at, but not proven. These three conditions are:

1) B does not occur until after A

2) A and B are related

3) Other explanations of the relationship between A and B can be ruled out.

What happens when we apply these criteria to Wade Boggs' elaborate behaviors? Boggs believes that his rituals (variable A) cause him to be a good hitter (variable B). In this case, Mill's first condition is met: B does not occur until after A. So far, so good. But can Boggs demonstrate that A and B are related? For example, is retracing his exact footprints as he runs to his position, or fielding exactly the same number of practice grounders in pre-game warm-up, necessary for him to hit well? Most likely, there is no relationship between these rituals and his batting ability. And given that the events aren't necessarily related, Mill's third condition cannot even be applied. So much for Boggs' beliefs.

How about Maria? In the situation where she systematically varied her smile, Maria meets Mills' three conditions: variable B (the sales) occurs after variable A (her smiling); she has determined that the two events are related; and, by controlling other factors, she has attempted to rule out other explanations for the relationship. However, in the second situation, in which Maria found a relationship between smiling and increased sales in retrospect after reading her diary, she can not meet Mills' first condition: she does not know if variable B followed variable A, or vice versa. Hence, she can not determine cause and effect.

Critical Thinking: General Principles and Case Studies

In your study of psychology, the distinction between correlation and causality will arise again and again. As a brief example, let's look at theories about the cause of schizophrenia, a mental disorder that involves serious disturbances in people's perceptions of reality and their ability to think and act rationally.

Although there is no cure for schizophrenia, the symptoms frequently can be alleviated by medication. The medication works by affecting a chemical in the brain called dopamine. By blocking the brain's receptor sites for dopamine, the drugs reduce the amount of dopaminergic (the adjective form of "dopamine") activity. Many people interpret this information to assume that an abnormality in dopamine functioning causes schizophrenia.

Yet such an assumption may be wrong. While the effects of the medication indicate that a relationship exists between dopamine and schizophrenia, the discovery of a relationship between two variables is not enough to prove causality. It may be, for example, that the drugs have some additional unknown effect that influences both dopamine functioning and schizophrenic symptoms. So at the current time, the best that can be said is that dopamine functioning is related to schizophrenia. The true cause (or, more accurately, causes) of schizophrenia remain unknown (Strauss & Carpenter, 1981).

By this point, you may be realizing that you have accumulated the wide array of knowledge that you hold in many different ways. Actually, very little of what we "know" personally is based on a rigorous scientific method. Some ideas we believe because of their tenacity. Others we believe because an authority figure has told us they are true. Still others we take for granted or assume to be true, without having challenged or tested them. And while it is not always feasible to conduct well-controlled experiments in our daily life, we <u>can</u> become more attentive to the fallacies and gaps in our own logical thinking. This can be accomplished by learning to think critically.

SOME PRINCIPLES OF CRITICAL THINKING

To learn to think critically, you need to familiarize yourself with four fundamental principles that characterize the process. Each of these principles can be thought of as a thinking skill or a set of related thinking capabilities. Honing these skills takes times and practice, but you may be surprised how quickly you can start mastering them and applying them to your course work, practical problems that arise in daily living, and your personal beliefs about complex social issues.

The four main principles that underlie critical thinking are: 1) identifying and challenging underlying assumptions; 2) checking for factual accuracy and logical consistency; 3) accounting for the importance of context; and 4) imagining and exploring alternatives. While we do not mean to suggest that this is an exhaustive list, or the only available strategy for learning critical thinking, these principles do lay a strong foundation for the critical evaluation of new information.

(1) Identifying and Challenging Assumptions

Every statement, every argument, every research proposition, no matter how factual or objective it may sound, has embedded within it certain assumptions. These assumptions may be quite subtle and difficult to recognize. Learning to identify and challenge the assumptions that underlie a statement is one of the most crucial components of critical thinking.

What do these assumptions consist of? They may be ideas that people take for granted, perhaps common sense beliefs that seem beyond questioning. Alternatively, they may represent values that you grew up with and that you believe are commonly shared, or they could be facts that you automatically accept as "given" without challenging them. Assumptions can be found in little truisms or proverbs that you find meaningful, in stereotypes, and in the beliefs that help create your views of life and the world.

Each of us has an enormous store of personal knowledge, some of which is shared by others, but much of which is unique to ourselves. This knowledge is an integral part of how we make sense of the world around us. Yet, when we stop and think about it, much of this "knowledge" is not factual, but based on beliefs and assumptions. We usually consider these beliefs self-evident, and only become aware of them through careful examination, or when they are challenged. This fund of information, sometimes called "implicit personal knowledge" or the "assumptive world" by psychologists, shapes our ideas and perceptions about the world (Janoff-Bulman, 1989; Polyani, 1962).

Identifying and challenging assumptions means two things, then. First, it involves looking at the assumptions that are hidden in somebody else's presentation of facts -- a speaker, an author, a classmate, a professor, a politician. Second, it means becoming aware of how our assumptions affect our own thinking. Our assumptions even act like a filter, guiding and shaping the information that we take in.

When presented with new information, or when examining their own ideas and beliefs about a topic, critical thinkers attempt to identify the assumptions that color and shape the information. Put simply, challenging assumptions means learning to separate opinion from fact. It is as if critical thinkers act like mental surgeons, operating on the facts they hear to "cut away" unwanted opinions and assumptions.

Even the statement "It's a beautiful day!" has an underlying assumption. (Before reading ahead, try to think about what it may be). If the day in question is sunny and warm with a gently billowing breeze, you may be likely to concur; in other words, you share with the speaker an assumption that weather of this sort is, indeed, "beautiful." It may seem such a factual and automatic response that you don't realize you are assuming anything. Yet the belief that such weather is "beautiful" is subjective, and represents an assumption.

Imagine, for example, that you have a friend for whom such "beautiful" days are extremely unpleasant. On cold and rainy days he is free to do as he pleases, but when the weather is temperate he must engage in laborious and tedious chores around the house. He dreads days that you consider beautiful, but feels joyous and carefree on rainy days. So when he greets you on a cold, damp day with a gleeful smile and a cheery "It sure is a beautiful day!," it becomes apparent that even simple interchanges about the weather can be clouded by underlying assumptions.

The fact that "It's a beautiful day" has a hidden assumption may seem to be relatively insignificant, and, on one level, it is. Critical thinking does not necessarily involve analyzing every casual sentence in conversation for flaws and hidden opinions. On a more complex level, though, assumptions about what is "right" influence our beliefs and actions on everything ranging from interpersonal relationships and how to spend leisure time to serious societal issues such as race relations, the environment, abortion, artificial parenthood, and on and on.

Additionally, identifying and challenging the assumptions that underlie statements of "fact" is often a crucial component of scientific progress. One example drawn from the field of psychology is how ideas about homosexuality have changed in the past two decades.

Until 1973, the American Psychiatric Association considered homosexuality a mental disorder. It no longer does. What is different now? Early psychological theories of homosexuality made the assumption that homosexuality was "abnormal" by adopting, without challenging, the prevalent cultural attitude. (The idea of homosexuality as abnormal is a good example of Peirce's method of tenacity; psychiatrists judged it to be deviant, in large part, because this had been a tenacious and long-standing belief in Western culture). But when researchers identified this as an assumption rather than fact, and designed experiments that set out to challenge the assumption, they found that a belief in the abnormality of homosexuality was unwarranted (see, e.g., Bell, Weinberg, & Hammersmith, 1981; Hooker, 1957, 1968; Saghir & Robins, 1971, 1973).

For example, in one study, psychiatrists looked at the results of psychological tests taken by homosexual and heterosexual men, without knowing whose test they were examining. The psychiatrists were then asked to determine which tests were those of gay men, and which were those of straight men. Until that time, psychiatrists had argued that homosexual men, because of their mental disturbance, could be distinguished from heterosexual men on the basis of psychological tests. However, the psychiatrists were unable to determine which tests had been taken by which group. In fact, the psychiatrists' performance was no better than chance (Hooker, 1957). Similarly, several other studies have been unable to distinguish gay and straight men on the basis of psychological functioning.

Therefore, the psychological community has moved away from the assumption that homosexuality is inherently disturbed. Still, because the method of tenacity is so strong, the culture at large sees this as a controversial issue. Remember the discussion of tenacity and schemas: It is only slowly that long-held beliefs are relinquished.

***

How can you learn to identify and challenge assumptions? To identify them, you can simply start by asking yourself what assumptions an author or speaker is making. (As an example, this booklet makes many assumptions, including the belief that critical thinking can be taught and is worth knowing. What other assumptions are being made)?

Yet this process of direct questioning is not always as simple as it sounds. To make it easier, try asking questions that are as specific as possible. Rather than looking at an overall topic and wondering if a specific conclusion is right or wrong, look at how the conclusion was derived. Ask yourself whether specific points represent "facts" or if they are assumptions. Remember, most statements of "fact" involve assumptions. These assumptions can be opinions, or they can be value judgments that inadvertently bias how the facts are presented.

To <u>challenge</u> assumptions after identifying them, ask yourself a different set of questions: Is this assumption justified, and is it reasonable? Why or why not? Do I agree with this assumption? What would happen if a different assumption was made?

Often, assumptions are uncovered when contradictions arise. Perhaps some new information or a new experience contradicts something you had previously believed. In such an instance, examine both the old and new information carefully, for you may discover that the discrepancy is based on differing assumptions. Similarly, if you read or hear something with which you disagree, this is a good clue that you and the author or speaker have differing assumptions underlying your viewpoints.

Finally, try to identify your own values and beliefs. Again, this is not as simple as it sounds. But as a exercise, spend a few minutes examining how you feel about a controversial social issue, such as abortion, surrogate motherhood, or capital punishment. After clarifying your stance, write down what you think is "fact" and what you think is "opinion." Then do the same thing with a topic in your daily life -- perhaps why someone should attend college, or what makes a good relationship. After you have done this for both topics, write down points of view that support the <u>opposite</u> position. (Don't cheat -- construct a good argument!) You may discover that your values and beliefs include many more assumptions and opinions than you had previously considered.

(2) <u>Checking for Factual Accuracy and Logical Consistency</u>

In addition to identifying and challenging hidden assumptions, critical thinkers examine the rationality of an argument or statement. This process involves two main questions: (1) how factually accurate is the information?; and (2) is the argument logical and consistent, or is there a fallacy in the reasoning?

<u>Checking for factual accuracy.</u> At its most basic level, checking for factual accuracy means verifying that information is true. Is the speaker/author making a clear and obvious factual error? Can the facts of an argument or statement be substantiated? What is the source of the information? In other words, critical thinkers pay careful attention to the evidence upon which an argument or claim is

being supported.

But checking for accuracy involves more than just verifying the validity of factual statements. Often, what is not said in a claim is as important as what is said. Facts can be distorted to mislead; they may be presented in such a way as to imply or suggest a conclusion that is unwarranted. When confronted with factual information, critical thinkers allow for the possibility that an important point might be missing from the presentation.

For example, a manufacturer proudly advertises that its brand of laundry detergent is "preferred by a 4:1 ratio." With such a claim, you are being led to believe that this product is the most popular and effective detergent. However, important information has been left out of the claim. Even if the 4:1 ratio is factually correct, with the specified product preferred four times as much, what is it being compared to? The advertiser doesn't say. It may be in comparison with other leading detergents, but it also may be compared to something that is an irrelevant or inappropriate basis of comparison. Because important information is missing, the claim is meaningless.

An incomplete presentation of facts, such as in the case above, is a common rhetorical devise. Politicians on the campaign trail, advertisers, lawyers trying to convince a jury --many persuasive individuals will use facts in a way that is technically not false, but nonetheless misleading. And the method isn't limited to people in authority; it is a frequently used technique to make something sound more factually based than it actually is.

A factual presentation of information can also be distorted by misusing charts and pictures. Often, a visual representation of an idea can help convey it clearly and succinctly. Graphs and charts can be used to clarify a topic that would otherwise be too cumbersome to express, but such visual props can also mislead.

Imagine, for example, that the number of applicants to a large state university has increased steadily and consistently over the past 7 years. In 1982, the school received 8,465 applications, and by 1989 the number of applicants had risen to 9,740. (This represents an increase of approximately 15% over the seven year span).

Now look at the three graphs on the next page (Figures 1, 2, and 3). They all present the same information: the university's steady increase of applicants over the seven years. But how different they look! Figure 1 presents what might seem to be the "truest" picture; visually, we read it as if a slight but steady increase has occurred. But by altering the relative dimensions of the graph (Figure 2) and the units of measurement (Figure 3), dramatically different pictures emerge, quite literally. While they all present the same "facts," the visual impact of each leads to different interpretations.

Similarly, graphs that don't tell you exactly what they are measuring are useless. For example, perhaps the manufacturers of the laundry detergent just discussed are eager to show how popular their brand has become. In advertisements, they use the graph shown in Figure 4 to demonstrate their increasing popularity. Very eye-catching and impressive...but meaningless, for they never state the unit of measurement. Each notch on the graph could

Figure 1
Number of Applicants to State U.

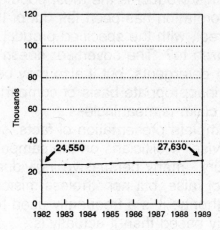

Figure 2
Number of Applicants to State U.

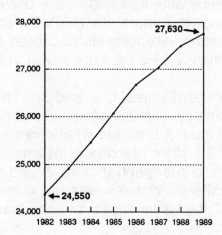

Figure 3
Number of Applicants to State U.

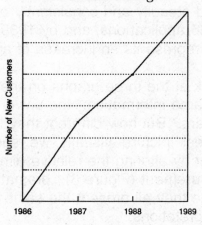

Figure 4
Increased Sales of "Our Brand" Detergent

Critical Thinking: General Principles and Case Studies

represent 50 new customers, or 50,000.

<u>Checking for logical consistency</u>. Sometimes, the facts of a claim may be correct and fully presented, with no deception and nothing omitted. Yet still a claim may be wrong.

After checking for accuracy, critical thinkers ask a second question: are the conclusions derived logically and consistently from the facts?

Suppose, for example, you were told about a study in which the aim was to test the concept of "penis envy". According to one highly controversial tenet of Sigmund Freud's theory of psychosexual development, females wish that they had a penis and feel envy towards people that have one.

The study went as follows: at the beginning of a college lecture, the researchers asked all the students, male and female, to fill out a questionnaire, and gave them each a pencil with which to do so. Actually, the questionnaire was irrelevant; the researchers were really interested in observing who would be more likely to keep the pencils, men or women. They found that significantly more men returned the pencils, and significantly more women kept them. The researchers speculated that the women kept the pencils because a pencil can be regarded as symbolic of a penis, and so stealing a pencil in fact represented a wish to have a penis. They therefore argued that their experiment supported the concept of penis envy.

Given what you already know about critical thinking, what do you think of this experiment? First, identify some of the assumptions being made. Can they be challenged? And second, does the conclusion derive logically from the data? It does not. While the information may be factually accurate -- the women may have kept the pencils more than the men -- the conclusion that this was due to penis envy does not necessarily follow.

One way to test the soundness of an argument's conclusions is to generate other explanations that would also fit the data. For example, perhaps more women kept the pencils because women carry pocketbooks and men don't. Perhaps women took more notes and wore down the points on the pencils, so chose not to return them. Perhaps it was chance, or some unknown additional factor, and the results wouldn't be the same in an experimental replication. Perhaps women do not have penis envy, but are inherently more dishonest than men (not a point substantiated by any research, mind you, but a possible alterative interpretation).

Critical thinkers also check for conclusions that are <u>tautological</u>. A tautology is a statement that is true by definition: Depressed people are sad. Good students achieve academic success. Fish are good swimmers because...well, because they're fish, so they have to be good swimmers. Such reasoning is circular because it "proves" what it is assumes to be true, but the "proof" is actually another example of the assumption.

Tautological reasoning is also used frequently in humor. An example is a joke Woody Allen tells in the movie <u>Annie Hall</u>: "My brother has a problem; he thinks he's a chicken. We'd take him to a psychiatrist ... except that we need the eggs." If you analyze the logic of the joke, you will find that it is based on the same tautological reasoning as the conclusion of the study.

One final way to think critically about whether a conclusion is accurately reached from a set of facts is to determine if a causal relationship has been inferred when only a correlation exists. Remember, as discussed previously, <u>correlation is not causality</u>. To prove causality between two variables is a specific and exacting process, but many correlational claims can misleadingly sound as if they are causal.

Take, for example, a study that relates back to the educational concept of formal discipline and the potential value of teaching Latin and Greek. A group of researchers in the early 1980s demonstrated that high school students who studied one of these two languages scored an average of 100 points higher on the verbal SAT than students who did not (cited in Lehman et al., 1988). Given these results, a newspaper editorial piece suggested that Latin or Greek should be taught to all students, because these dramatic results indicated that studying one of these languages obviously helped make pupils smarter (Costa, 1982).

Can you identify the editorialist's mistake? He took two bits of information that were related -- studying Latin or Greek, and a high SAT score -- and assumed that one caused the other. It sounds plausible, yet such an assumption is unjustified and quite possibly mistaken.

For example, it may be that only exceptional students decided to study Latin or Greek in the first place; in that case, they may have excelled on the SATs regardless of studying the language. It may also be that schools that offered Latin or Greek courses were generally of a higher academic caliber than schools that did not, and actually taking Latin or Greek was less important than attending a school that offered these courses. Whatever the reason (or, more likely, combination of reasons), a critical thinker would dismiss the editorialist's claim because the conclusion is not logically derived from the evidence.

In summary, checking for factual accuracy and logical consistency involves asking yourself several questions. Are the facts accurate, and verifiable? Is important information missing, so that the facts that are presented are misleading? Does an argument or statement make logical sense? Is a conclusion based on circular (tautological) reasoning -- in other words, is it defining its answer in terms of its unquestioned assumptions? And finally, can it be demonstrated that one event caused another to happen, or are they only related to one another?

(3) <u>Considering the Importance of Context</u>

A recent book on creative problem solving offers the following puzzling "letter" (Bransford & Stein, 1984, p. 51):

> Dear Jill,
>   Remember Sally, the person I mentioned in my last
> letter? You'll never guess what she did this week. First,
> she let loose a team of gophers. The plan backfired
> when a dog chased them away. She then threw a party,
> but the guests failed to bring their motorcycles.

Furthermore, her stereo system was not loud enough. Sally spent the next day looking for a "Peeping Tom," but was unable to find one in the yellow pages. Obscene phone calls gave her some hope until the number was changed. It was the installation of blinking neon lights across the street that finally did the trick. Sally framed the ad from the classified section and now has it hanging on her wall.

Love,
Bill

Reading this letter, it is difficult to comprehend what Bill is trying to communicate. The words make sense, as do the sentences. Grammatically the writing is fine, but what does it mean? Is it simply gibberish?

The meaning of the letter becomes much clearer when one understands the context of Sally's unusual actions: she dislikes her next-door neighbors and wants them to move away. Knowing this, go back and read the letter again. While you might not approve of her devious schemes, the meaning of her behavior is much more comprehensible!

Appreciating the importance of contextual information is a primary feature of critical thinking. Ideas are rarely context-free; the same "fact" or set of facts can have tremendously different meanings in different contexts. A child shrieking at the top of her lungs, for example, could indicate that she feels great distress -- but if she is at an amusement park, sandwiched into a roller-coaster car with her best friends and careening down the track at breakneck speed, it could signify utter delight. Similarly, getting a "C" on an exam could be terribly disappointing to a student accustomed to earning straight A's, but a welcome sign of progress for a student who regularly fails his courses.

Psychologists are well aware of the importance of context in determining human behavior. For example, in a series of classic experiments, Asch (1951) demonstrated the enormous effect of the social influence of peers, even on such matters as how people perceive unambiguous visual stimuli. Asch's experiments are important because they reveal the extreme influence of context: if you are in a room full of people, all of whom perceive something differently than you, you are apt to change your perception to match theirs. Psychologists have also demonstrated that how people respond to "emergency" situations also varies significantly, depending upon the context of the emergency (e.g. Darley & Latané, 1968; Latané & Darley, 1976).

When presented with new information or ideas, then, critical thinkers ask themselves in what context (or contexts) the information makes sense. They consider if the information applies universally, in every situation, or if it only applies in very specific circumstances. In addition, they try to determine if are there cases in which the facts do not apply -- where, in fact, the same facts mean something else.

The importance of context in determining the validity of a proposition also suggests that absolute or dogmatic statements should be treated with extreme caution. Sentences that begin with "People always..." or "It is never the case that..." usually ignore the importance of the context in which the supposed "always" or "never" takes place. Furthermore, many sentences don't explicitly state the "always" or "never," but imply it between the lines. Critical thinkers try to hear when an absolute claim is being implied and then sort out the contexts and situations in which the claim may be true.

As an example of ignoring the importance of context, consider proverbs. With catchy phrasing and a succinct message, the lessons that proverbs teach are easy to learn. But if you think for a moment about the proverbs you know, you may discover that for each "truth" a proverb reveals, a second proverb offers a "truth" exactly opposite the first!

For example, a well-known saying tells us that "absence makes the heart grow fonder" -- but an equally popular proverb warns us "out of sight, out of mind." And we all know that "too many cooks spoil the broth," but at the same time, "many hands make light work." And imagine how difficult it is to live boldly, since "opportunity knocks only once" and "nothing ventured, nothing gained," while simultaneously trying to live cautiously, because "it is better to be safe than sorry." (Try to think of some more pairs of proverbs that offer opposing and contradictory "truths.")

Critical thinkers are wary of proverbial sayings because they leave out as much as they include, failing to take context into account. Most proverbs do have some wisdom to offer regarding the human condition, but they present only part of the picture. Taken individually, any proverb is incomplete because it offers its "truth" in a more absolute manner than actually fits the wide breadth of human functioning (listen for the implied "always" or "never" that remains hidden).

Cultural Relativity. So far, the importance of context has been discussed in terms of identifying different meanings for the same facts and in rejecting the absolutism of all-or-none claims. One more feature is necessary to appreciate the importance of context for critical thinking: the cultural relativity of ideas.

It may be difficult to imagine that many of the ideas and beliefs that you hold as important are not universal, but are instead shaped and defined by cultural influences. When considering their core beliefs, people tend to feel that all individuals must feel the same way or that their beliefs must be absolute rather than relative. Yet, many of the ideas we hold, the actions we take, and the emotions we display are shaped by cultural guidelines and expectations.

For example, consider how people grieve in response to the death of a loved one. Our culture has many unstated "rules", or social norms, regarding how to mourn the death of a loved person. These norms include such things as who is permitted (or expected) to grieve, how long the period of grief should last, what emotions the grieving person can display, and how the bereaved person should act. Imagine how odd it might seem for a man who was recently widowed to be laughing and cavorting about in public, or parents who had recently lost a child to mourn for four days and then never publicly mention their child again, or a recently

Critical Thinking: General Principles and Case Studies

widowed woman to take a knife and inflict wounds on herself.

Yet, these mourning practices are considered normal in others cultures. Although crying appears to be the most common cross-cultural response to the death of a loved one, in Balinese society, bereaved individuals never cry in public. Instead, they act in a friendly and jovial nature (Rosenblatt, Walsh & Jackson, 1976). The Hopi Indians of North America have a grief period of four days, after which the bereaved person is expected to return to the tasks of daily life and make no mention of the departed person (Miller & Schoenfeld, 1973). And self-infliction of injury is a mourning ritual practiced in several cultures (see Pollock, 1972, for a review). From the perspectives of these other cultures, crying in public, elaborate mourning rituals, or acting depressed for many months after a loss seems unusual and "abnormal."

For a person who is grieving in our culture, the emotional experience of grief may seem so dramatic and vivid that it does not seem shaped by cultural rules. Yet grieving must be culturally-shaped, given the evidence that other cultures handle loss differently. To understand a psychological phenomenon such as grief, then, it is important to think critically about the cultural context in which it occurs and to determine how one's own ideas and beliefs about the phenomenon might be defined by one's own culture.

(4) Imagining and Exploring Alternatives

So far, we've discussed the importance of several skills for critical thinking: 1) identifying and challenging assumptions in your own thinking and that of an author or speaker; 2) checking for factual accuracy and logical consistency; and 3) taking into account the context of a set of facts. But these guidelines are only part of the picture. They all require you to act somewhat like a strict interrogator; your task is to detect flaws in logic, uncover lurking opinions, debunk erroneous assertions, and reject claims that are too extreme. A fourth component of critical thinking, imagining and exploring alternative solutions, calls instead for creative ingenuity. In many situations, it is not enough simply to point out the shortcomings or inconsistencies in an idea or argument; critical thinking also involves generating new ideas, alternative explanations, and more viable solutions than those that are presented.

Like the other components of critical thinking, the skills involved in generating creative and fresh alternatives can be honed through practice. The following strategies will help you develop the ability to imagine and explore creative alternatives to problems.

1. Simplify complex information.

It is obviously helpful to have a full grasp on a problem or issue before tackling it. However, complex topics are, by definition, difficult to understand. Cognitive psychologists have demonstrated that there is a limited amount of material a person can comprehend at once; it is easy to get "overloaded" by too much information. Therefore, when presented with a barrage of facts, or when you feel there is too much information to easily make sense of, try organizing it into a simpler form before generating alternative ideas.

One way to simplify complex information is to systematically break it down into component parts. If you play a musical instrument, for example, you probably have a different approach to learning an easy piece of music than to learning one that is long and challenging. With an easy piece, you may try sight-reading it, playing the whole composition at once. But with a more complex piece, you would likely try to learn it a bit at a time. You might concentrate on one movement or section until you have mastered that and then go on to the next section. Only after approaching it in its components might you attempt to interpret or understand it as an entire piece.

The same principle can be applied to complex ideas. It is often helpful to divide a large problem into simpler components, making sense of them individually before attempting to master the larger phenomenon. And it is often easier to think of changes at the component level of a problem than confronting it as a whole.

A second strategy to simplify information is to visualize it. Rather than hold a complex problem in your head, write out its components. For example, make a list of "pros and cons" or "strengths and weaknesses" of a proposition, and compare the two. Or, perhaps the information lends itself well to charts or other pictorial representations. Sometimes it is helpful to write an outline of an argument or idea, to be able to "see" if the logic is consistent.

Because organizing complex information into a visual model simplifies it, it helps you to imagine and explore alternatives. To further generate new ideas, after organizing the information, try to organize it again -- differently. Any pie can be sliced in a number of ways; what happens when you take the same information, but organize it in a different method?

A third way of simplifying complex information is to try to understand it by means of an analogous everyday example. Bring things into your own frame of reference. This might mean substituting simple words for complicated scientific or technical language. It might mean thinking of an experience you've had that typifies a larger concept. Or it might involve providing specific details to an idea that is only presented as an abstraction.

For example, imagine the following problem. Four cards are placed in front of you displaying an A, a B, a 4 and a 7. Every card has a letter on the front and a number on the back. Your instructions are to turn over only the cards necessary to establish this rule: if there is a vowel on the front, then there is an even number on the back. What cards do you turn over?

Most adults do not correctly complete this task (Wason, 1966). However, here is an analogous example, with more familiar, less abstract terms (D'Andrade, 1982). Instead of four cards, you have four receipts. Two are facing up: one for $25, the other for $15. The other two face down: one has a signature, the other one does not. Your instructions are to turn over only the receipts necessary to establish that if a receipt is for more than $20, then it has a signature on the back. Which receipts do you turn over?

Critical Thinking: General Principles and Case Studies

If you answered that you need to turn over two receipts -- the one for $25 (to make sure it is signed) and the receipt that is unsigned (to make sure it is not for an amount larger than $20) you reasoned correctly. By similar logic, with the first task you need to turn over the A and the 7. When the same conceptual problem is applied in more familiar terms, subjects find the second task easier than the first (D'Andrade, 1982).

2. Redefine the problem.

Redefining a problem involves trying to look at it from a fresh perspective. Often, a problem and its components have been defined in a certain way. What happens if those definitions are stretched, altered, or abandoned altogether? Trying to conceptualize a problem or argument from different vantage points can lead to new ideas.

For example, in one experimental situation, subjects were presented with a candle, a large box of matches, and several thumbtacks (Duncker, 1945). Their task was to mount the candle on the wall so that it could be used for illumination. No other tools or objects could be used. How could this be done? (Sorry -- the thumbtacks were not big enough to fit through the candle).

Most subjects were unable to figure out how to accomplish the task. But there is a simple solution, which involves redefining the possible function of one of the objects: the matchbox. By emptying out the matches, the box can be tacked to the wall, and converted into a candle holder.

What many people fail to see in approaching this situation is that the matchbox can be used as anything other than a matchbox. This is an example of a phenomenon called <u>functional fixedness</u>: it is difficult to look at familiar objects in a novel or unfamiliar way.

The same is true when approaching complex problems. We often become locked into seeing something from only one perspective or vantage point. However, overcoming this "cognitive fixedness" can allow us to creatively explore solutions to problems with ideas that otherwise would not have occurred to us.

3. Brainstorming.

Brainstorming is usually thought of as a group activity. However, the principles involved can also be practiced by a single individual attempting to imagine and explore novel solutions to problems.

The technique of brainstorming (Osborn, 1963) begins by defining a problem that needs to be addressed. After the problem is defined, the next step is to think of as many solutions as possible, with one important condition: the newly generated ideas are not critiqued or judged. For brainstorming to be effective, it is necessary to temporarily suspend the immediate judgments that new suggestions sometimes elicit. There are no such things as "good" ideas or "bad" ideas in brainstorming. No matter how seemingly outlandish, far-fetched, or insignificant, all possible solutions or redefinitions of the problem are encouraged.

As you might guess, the purpose of brainstorming is to overcome or circumvent some of the other problems that have already been discussed. By generating new ideas in a way that encourages creativity and novelty, ideas may germinate and take root that would otherwise be quickly dismissed. Even the most preposterous suggestion may have within it a kernel of truth or the key to unravelling a knotty problem.

After the new ideas have been generated in a judgement-free manner, they are then evaluated one by one to determine their helpfulness. In this process, the evaluation proceeds as does the evaluation of any new ideas or propositions: with the guidelines for critical thinking already discussed.

4. Switching roles.

One of the ways we mentioned to simplify a complex argument was to write it down. Not only does this allow you to visually organize the material, it can also help you try to reconstruct and understand the logic of a different viewpoint.

When you are presented with an idea or an argument with which you disagree, or that you can not follow, try to construct, step by step, how authors or speakers have reached their conclusions. Try to follow their logic, attempting to see the situation from their eyes. Imagine that you have to agree with, and defend, their conclusion in a debate; how would you convince somebody of their point?

In the process of hypothesizing how someone reached a conclusion other than your own, several things may happen. You may uncover questionable assumptions in their (or your) logic. You may be able to isolate specifically where the point of disagreement is. And, in a creative way, you may be able to take the strongest points of both arguments and forge a new, flexible alternative.

As we mentioned earlier, a valuable exercise is to spend a few moments looking at a social issue that you have strong feelings about, but imagining that you need to defend the opposite view from the one you hold. (Most complex issues have adherents on either side, many of whom have struggled with their choices). Can you identify the differing assumptions in the different views, and come up with any novel solutions?

***

These strategies are just a few of the several ways to creatively explore alternative options. The process of creating new possibilities goes hand in hand with the other steps of critical thinking; after potential alternatives are generated, they can be subject to the same critical scrutiny as any other proposition.

One impediment to critical thinking is an overly strong attachment to one's own ideas. (People often find it easier to practice the skills of critical thinking in dissecting someone else's argument than to think critically about their own views.) But critical thinkers maintain the same questioning attitude towards their own ideas as towards those of others. They approach all ideas, both their own and others', with a stance of "reflective skepticism" (Brookfield, 1987), meaning that they greet all challenging ideas or information with serious, but cautious, consideration.

When people learn to relinquish their investment in the rigid maintenance of their own beliefs, they can also allow for a potentially valuable source of new information: making mistakes. Part of imagining and exploring creative options is learning from things that have gone wrong. In sum, don't be discouraged or disheartened about having made mistakes; use them as an education.

<u>A Final Comment on the Principles of Critical Thinking</u>

These four principles -- identifying and challenging assumptions, checking for factual accuracy and logical consistency, looking at context, and imagining and exploring alternatives -- form the foundation of critical thinking. Taken together, these guidelines will help you think critically about information you learn in school, read in the newspaper, hear on television, or glean from casual conversations with friends or family. They will assist you in examining some of your own ethical positions on difficult social problems. And these guidelines can even help win arguments with your friends!

Critical thinking will also help you evaluate the merits of research, as you encounter it in academic settings and in the culture in general. It is to this application of critical thinking that we now turn our attention.

THINKING CRITICALLY TO EVALUATE RESEARCH

We live in a research-oriented society. From the pioneering breakthroughs on the cutting edge of medical science to the semi-annual choices network executives agonize over regarding what television programs to air, research is a fact of modern life. We rely on it, and with this reliance comes an inherent danger, for research findings can be easily misused, distorted, or taken out of context to say something other than what they are meant to.

Thinking critically goes hand in hand with developing an appreciation of the enormous benefits, and inherent dangers, of scientific research. Research is a double-edged sword; when misapplied, its ability to obscure knowledge is as great as its ability to illuminate. Research that is soundly conducted can answer difficult questions with more certainty and objectivity than any other method of inquiry, but the casual reporting of research can be fraught with distortions that, intentionally or unintentionally, mislead an unsuspecting public. Studies may be poorly designed or conducted, findings can be taken out of context and misapplied, and "results" can be carefully worded so as to subtly, but wrongly, imply the truthfulness of a dubious claim.

As we've already mentioned, the field of psychology has as one of its cornerstones a commitment to empiricism, or the research-based validation of its concepts. As such, the study of psychology is a particularly helpful context in which to hone your skills of assessing and evaluating the merits of research.

Psychologists say many things about human nature, based on the research they conduct. However, rather than believing something simply because a psychologist says it (beware the method of authority), critical thinkers carefully scrutinize research to determine, for themselves, how sound it is.

Six steps characterize the research process in the field of psychology (Winter, personal communication). Each step is associated with particular issues relevant to critical thinking.

Step 1: The Idea

Psychological research begins with an idea. This idea may relate to a practical or societal problem that needs a solution. It may be a casual observation of human behavior that warrants closer examination. Conversely, it may be derived from a specific theory and represent a test of the theory's power to predict certain outcomes.

Applying Critical Thinking:

When assessing a single experiment or a program of research (a series of studies that are unified by the same theme), first try to identify the underlying idea or theory on which the experimenter is basing his or her study. What are some of the assumptions the experimenter is making? If the idea for the study is derived from a larger theory, is it logically consistent with the theory? If the study relates to a social or practical problem, is the problem being defined in a way that makes sense? Is the context of the problem being taken into account?

Step 2: The Question

The researcher's idea leads to the development of a specific question. This question, sometimes stated as a formal hypothesis, should be framed in a way that allows it to be tested -- in other words, it has to be asked so that it can be answered, so that the experiment will support or negate it.

Applying Critical Thinking:

First, identify as specifically as possible the question that is being asked in the experiment. After you have identified it, ask yourself if this question is logically derived from the idea that guides the experiment and is a testable (answerable) question. Further, consider if the way in which the question is framed introduces any hidden assumptions about what the outcome of the study will be. Is the experimenter introducing any bias into the study?

Step 3: The Method

To answer the question, the experimenter devises a scientific method that "translates" the question into a research procedure. By developing an experimental model or a means of systematic observation, the experimenter attempts to answer the experimental question as accurately and specifically as possible

Applying Critical Thinking:

Again, the first step is to identify the procedure that the experimenter has employed to test the question. Does the approach make sense to you? Is it logically derived from, and consistent with, the experimental question?

In the leap from hypothetical question to experimental design, research studies can sometimes develop a crucial gap in logic. In some cases, a laboratory-designed study does not accurately capture the "real world" phenomenon it is trying to examine, and so the results of the study, however interesting, will be of little relevance to the original situation. At other times, a research design may introduce new variables that inadvertently distort the experimental question. In these cases, the results can not be associated, with certainty, with the original question of interest.

Thus, two crucial questions must be asked of any research design: 1) Does the research design adequately capture the real world phenomenon or theoretical concept that it is attempting to examine? 2) Has the design introduced any unwanted and irrelevant features that distort the experimental question?

Step 4: The Experiment

Once an experimenter has an idea, a testable question, and a procedure to test the question, the next step is to conduct an initial experiment. The results of the experiment will confirm or refute the question asked.

Applying Critical Thinking:

At this step in the process, critical thinking follows two paths. First, are the results accurate? Are they presented in a complete and detailed manner, without any significant omissions or gaps in logic?

Second, are the results being presented in an appropriate context? Or has the experimenter taken accurate results, but applied them in a way that extends beyond the limitations of the experimental design? Remember that the results relate to the experimental situation, but not necessarily the "real world." Are the results reported in a fashion that is too global, too inclusive, or too absolute?

It is also important to consider the results in the context of other scientific inquiries on the same topic. Single studies seldom prove a point decisively, and it is rare for scientific progress to hinge on a single, monumental experiment. In most cases knowledge accrues slowly, as consistent research findings gradually accumulate. Therefore, when faced with the results of a single study, critical thinkers ask themselves: What is not being reported? Are these results consistent and expected with what is already known, or is this the only study to produce the results it did, whereas many others produced opposing results?

Step 5: Criticism

After the results of an initial study are made known, the next step in the research process is criticism.

Other members of the scientific community examine the study and its conclusions. The criticisms might focus on the experimental design or methodology (in which case, they would echo the critical questions discussed above). Frequently, other researchers will question not the results themselves, but how the experimenter explains or interprets them. Approaching the same experimental phenomenon from a different angle, or with a different theoretical idea, other researchers will propose alternative explanations for the findings.

Applying Critical Thinking:

Researchers do not present experimental results in a vacuum: they also explain what they think the results mean or indicate. At this step, then, think critically not only about the results, but also about the explanation offered for them. Does the explanation make sense? Is it the only possible explanation for those results? If not, could you generate alterative explanations?

Also important at this stage of the process is carefully examining the assumptions that are embedded in the explanation. Probably more so here than at any other point in the scientific process, assumptions can be uncovered that affect the interpretation of the results. What is the researcher presenting as fact that might be an opinion or a personally held, subjective value?

Step 6: Further Studies

After other researchers suggest alternative explanations for the results, they in turn conduct <u>further studies</u> to support or disconfirm the new interpretations. In this manner, the cycle of research and the gradual accrual of knowledge continues. Previous findings are either replicated or refuted, new findings lead to new questions, which in turn beget new findings, and old theories are strengthened, modified, or discarded.

Applying Critical Thinking:

Often at this point in the scientific process, different researchers will argue that the same facts mean entirely different things. To think critically, evaluate the different explanations. Do they make sense individually? Is one better than the others? Why or why not? Can you synthesize differing points of view to generate a creative new alternative?

Earlier, we mentioned that psychology is a discipline that looks at phenomena at different levels of analysis, from the microscopic to the molar. Is there a way in which differing explanations could be approaching the same phenomenon at varying levels of analysis? If so, how could one or more views be integrated?

Understanding and practicing these guidelines for critically evaluating research will help you in your introduction to the field of psychology. But, in all likelihood, the gain will extend beyond that. Pick up a newspaper, turn on the radio, watch the advertisements on television -- the casual reporting of research findings permeates our culture. And the more you know about the mechanics of sound research, the more mental ammunition you'll have to determine, for yourself, what research claims you choose, or choose not to, believe.

A FEW CONCLUDING COMMENTS

Earlier in this booklet, we mentioned that the skills of critical thinking can be likened to a cognitive tool-kit. Tools take time to master; anyone can hold a hammer, but only with practice can you learn to hit a nail consistently on the head. So it is, too, with the critical thinking skills discussed here. Don't be discouraged if you don't immediately fully integrate these guidelines into your style of thinking and become a critical thinking "whiz." With time, patience and practice, you can develop your ability to think critically. These guidelines can become a familiar, and useful, means of evaluating new information.

Teaching students to think critically is currently a major focus of higher education, and we do not suggest that the system presented here is the definitive one, or that it is the only way for you to learn critical thinking skills. But we do believe that the four principles we discuss -- identifying and challenging assumptions, checking for factual accuracy and logical consistency, accounting for the importance of context, and imagining and exploring alternatives -- provide a strong foundation. These guidelines can strengthen your ability to evaluate factual-sounding claims made by professors, friends, politicians, and advertisers. They can also help you clarify your personal beliefs on difficult social topics, and judge fairly those beliefs that differ from your own.

One final note: critical thinking can be fun. Rather than approaching these skills as a burdensome task, think instead of the pleasure associated with implementing a creative new idea, solving a complex problem, or understanding, for the first time, an idea that had always mystified you. Broadening one's intellectual abilities can be enormously rewarding in its own right, and critical thinking can be a valuable source of intellectual enrichment, personal growth, and pride in your own cognitive abilities.

II. CASE STUDIES

Calisthenics for Critical Thinkers

Now that you have your toolbox, it's time to get to work. For in the case of learning to think critically, the old adage "practice makes perfect" could not be more appropriate. Just as muscles atrophy and lose their strength if not worked out, critical thinking "muscles" also grow weak if not exercised.

The remainder of this book is designed to let you try out your new tools, and to build up the muscles necessary to use them. What you will find in the following pages are case studies about everyday people doing everyday activities. In each story, you will see how the psychological concepts and phenomenon (which you are reading and learning about in class) affect people's behavior in all kinds of ways. These stories cover a wide range of topics and issues that are central to contemporary psychology.

After reading each story, you will be asked to apply your growing knowledge of psychology to understanding the events the story chronicles. This is where you will put your critical thinking skills to work. While not all of the questions require deep contemplative thought, many questions will challenge you to reconsider your old beliefs about human behavior. Some questions may also challenge the assumptions of the psychology that you are learning.

But these case studies serve another purpose as well. Before you can think critically about a body of information, you must first understand it. After all, how can you evaluate something that you do not fully comprehend? The second purpose of these case studies, then, is to help you develop a better understanding of contemporary psychology.

One of the things that many students new to psychology find difficult when learning about the field is the variable level at which phenomenon are discussed. At times you will be learning about large theories that attempt to explain all human behavior, and you may wonder how to account for smaller specific behaviors. At other times specific behaviors will be the focus of discussion, and you may then find yourself asking how this fits into the bigger picture. In other words, psychology sometimes focuses on forests and sometimes on trees. It will be important for you to occasionally step back and see the forests despite the trees, and at other times to step forward and focus on the trees ignoring the forest.

Before you answer the questions that accompany each story, make sure you have read the appropriate section of your textbook or have gone over the material in class. In addition, remind yourself of how a critical thinker would approach the questions. By keeping in mind how a critical thinker considers problems, you will get the most out of these case studies.

You are now ready to begin applying critical thinking to psychology. Good Luck!

1. Introduction to the Field and Research Methods - The Fields of Psychology

"Hey, Benny, are you finished with the sports section?" asked Celia of her office-mate Ben. The two had shared an office in the computer science department for two years, and shared a subscription to the daily newspaper.

"Almost, Celia. Hey, did you hear about this soccer riot in England? Why does this kind of thing always happen at soccer games? You never hear about fights breaking out at pro football or basketball games."

"I don't know Ben. I guess the British love their soccer. Of course, how would I have heard about the riot when you've had the sports section for the past 30 minutes!"

"Yeah, yeah. I'm almost finished." Ben turned to the last page only to find a half-page ad announcing a huge sale on all tires in stock, and another reminding readers that winter was approaching and encouraging them to take their cars in for tune-ups and fresh anti-freeze.

"Here you go, Celia," he said handing the sports section over to her. "You know, if I'd known you were such a big sports fan, I wouldn't have agreed to share this newspaper subscription with you in the first place."

1)   In general, more men than women probably read sports sections of newspapers. What branches of psychology might address this and other gender differences in behavior?

2)   Consider the soccer riot that Ben read about in the paper. What types of questions might a social psychologist ask about the occurrence of such group phenomenon? What types of questions might a personality psychologist ask? What types of questions might a cross-cultural psychologist ask?

3)   Do you think that the placement of car ads in the sports page is coincidental? What branch of psychology might have informed the advertisers of such products?

4)   Witnessing a riot can be psychologically damaging. What branch of psychology would try to help individuals trying to cope with the trauma of such an event? What is the difference between counseling psychology and clinical psychology?

5)   Have you ever considered how complicated a process reading a newspaper is? Can you identify which branch of psychology tries to understand the mental processes involved in reading? Which branch may address how children's develop reading skills?

Critical Thinking: General Principles and Case Studies

2. Introduction to the Field and Research Methods - The Models of Psychology

Snapping on the TV and flipping to Oprah, Cheryl looked at her watch. It was 4:15. She had missed the beginning and would have to try to catch up.

On stage, two "experts" argued over why people fall in love. The first speculated about what elements of another person we fell in love with. Did we fall in love with a face, or with a pair of eyes, or with some facet of another's personality? The second "expert" maintained that it was impossible to separate individual features. "It is the whole person with whom we fall in love," he said.

Then came comments from the audience. One audience member commented that only after people rose above everyday concerns and worries were they capable of experiencing true love. A second audience member firmly believed people are innately driven to love certain types of others and that love was a biological not psychological response. A third person claimed that people fall in love with people who remind them of their parents. Finally, a fourth person argued that to understand why someone was in love you had to "see the world through their eyes."

1)   With what school of psychological thought is Wilhelm Wundt associated? What method did he suggest for understanding human thoughts and behaviors? With which of the two love experts would he have sided?

2)   Describe the Gestalt approach to understanding psychological phenomenon. Which person in this narrative is expressing most clearly the ideas of this school of thought?

3)   Describe the humanistic model of psychology. What would this model suggest about the first audience member's comment about love? What would this model suggest about the third audience member's comment?

4)   Which models of psychology are most interested with the "inner mind?" What would these models think about the second audience member's comment?   About the fourth audience member's comment?

Critical Thinking: General Principles and Case Studies

"Thanks again for coming on such short notice, Sue," Lee said appreciatively as she shut the car door. Lee and Brad Johnson were afraid that they'd have to cancel their dinner plans when their usual babysitter called at the last minute to cancel. Fortunately, Brad was able to convince Sue to take her place.

Lee usually wouldn't have asked Sue to babysit; Sue had a bad habit of staying on the phone half the night and letting the television do the babysitting for her. "Brad, do you ever get concerned that Sue lets the kids watch too much TV?"

"I really don't think one night is going to hurt them; but I really don't think any of those police shows are good for them. I think that kids who watch even one of those shows start to think that crime is normal. I think they start to care about others less, and to be less compassionate to people in trouble."

"Maybe we should call her and tell her that when we get to the Rineharts," Lee suggested, "that is, if she's not on the phone already."

1) What is a theory? What is Brad's theory of the effects of television on children?

2) What is a hypothesis that might come from Brad's theory? Can you think of an experiment design to test his theory?

3)   Lee read in a news magazine that children who watched more violent shows tended to be less compassionate. The researchers concluded that parents should not let their children watch police shows. Evaluate their conclusion.

4)   Lee suggests investigating their theory by studying their own children? What kind of research is this? What are the drawbacks to their method? What are the advantages?

5)   Brad is curious to know how much television children in their neighborhood watch. To find out he called twenty of his friends and asked them how much TV they let their children watch. What is this type of research called? What are the advantages and disadvantages of this type of research in general? What are the drawbacks to Brad's approach in general?

4. Introduction to the Field and Research Methods - Methods of Research II

Doug is a psychology major beginning his senior year. As part of his degree requirement, Doug must design and conduct an experiment. Being interested in persuasion, he decides to investigate possible personality variables he believes might be associated with the ability to resist being persuaded by others.

Asking his subjects to administer increasingly large shocks to a laboratory rat, Doug recorded how far he is able to persuade each person to carry the shocks. He then compared this measure to several personality scales, including a measure of aggressiveness that was obtained by recording the highest level of shock administered to the rat. Surprisingly, this measure of persuasion is correlated positively with authoritarianism and aggressiveness; and negatively with vegetarianism and self-esteem. Doug concludes that aggressive and authoritative individuals are more likely to follow orders, whereas vegetarians are less likely to follow orders.

1)   What is the dependent variable in this study? How is this variable operationalized? Are there any problems with this operationalization?

2)   Are the conclusions that both aggressive and authoritative individuals are more likely to follow orders a good ones? Defend your answer. Of which conclusion can we be more certain?

3)   Consider the conclusion that vegetarians are less likely to follow orders. What important fact is Doug overlooking in making this conclusion?

4)   When discussing the implication of this study for teaching people to be resistant to persuasion, Doug suggests by increasing self-esteem, one can increase resistance to unwanted persuasion. Is this a reasonable implication of this study?

5. Introduction to the Field and Research Methods - Methods of Research III

For the second time in four weeks, Amy won the football pool by picking the most winning teams for the week. This wouldn't have been so frustrating for Jon except for one thing: Amy knows next to nothing about football.

"I don't understand how you do it Amy, but I'm going to figure it out."

"I told you before. I've always been kinda' psychic about things. My mom is the same way. In fact, I think it runs in our family. Maybe it's genetic."

Jon and Amy had had this argument a dozen times. In fact, such an argument inspired a psychology project collaboration between them. Each asked twenty people if they had ever had a psychic experience. Oddly, while only one of the people Jon interviewed reported having such experiences, five of twenty told Amy about a psychic experience.

"Yeah, maybe it's genetic," Jon said returning to the conversation. "Or maybe you're just lucky."

1) Is the number of people who reported to Amy having had a psychic experience meaningfully higher than the number of people who reported this to Jon? How do psychologists determine if differences such as this are meaningful?

2) Suppose that the difference in reported psychic experiences is meaningful, could this be the result of some type of bias? How do psychologists combat such biases?

3)   Does the procedure Jon and Amy choose to use truly illuminate the issue of whether the possible source of Amy's success is due to genetic factors?

4)   Many studies have been conducted testing the validity of ESP. How might a psychologists draw conclusions on the basis of this large body of research?

6. Biology Underlying Behavior - The Brain and the Nervous System I

On Friday evenings Bob liked to join his friends at the Anchor, a pub style bar near campus. The Anchor has a wide selection of beers on tap as well as bottled beer from 30 countries on six continents (Antarctica having yet to produce a malt beverage). This Friday was no exception. After enjoying two beers at home to start the evening, Bob made the short walk to the Anchor. As it turned out, his friends Kathy and Sean were there celebrating; their English literature class had a mid-term exam that afternoon and both had to study all week to get ready. As the night, and the drinking, progressed, Bob's behavior began to change in predictable ways: his speech became slurred, his balance began to go, and his thinking became narrowly focused. Additionally, many social inhibitions were shed and Bob approached people and made statements he never would have when sober.

1) Which of Bob's drinking-behaviors are associated to the "new brain"? Which are associated with the "old-brain"?

2) Why did alcohol consumption affect Bob's ability to walk with a normal, smooth balance? What region of his brain was affected and in what ways?

3)   What physiological effects does alcohol consumption have on the body's neurotransmitters? Can these effects be traced to any quality that is characteristic of drunkenness? Which qualities?

4)   Alcohol is often called a depressant. However, most people who drink that it does not "depress" them. In what way then is alcohol a depressant? Can you postulate any physiological basis for alcohol induced affects on mood?

7. Biology Underlying Behavior - The Brain and Nervous System II

Returning from winter break, Pat was disappointed to discover that she had gained seven pounds. Reasoning that it had taken a month to gain the weight, she resolved to begin a one month regimen of diet and exercise. In a symbolic gesture, Pat dug out a pair of running shoes that had not been worn in six months. Changing into grey sweats, she was ready to go. After briefly stretching her leg muscles she headed toward the student union. The union building was three quarters of a mile and she reasoned that the mile and a half run would be a good length for her first day. But it wasn't long before Pat noticed a slight pain in her stomach, and now she remembered why she had given up jogging six months ago - abdominal cramps. Slight at first, the cramps increased noticeably as she crossed Memorial Bridge at the west gate of campus. Approaching the student union, she felt certain that she was not going to be able to complete her trip. Unexpectedly, just as she circled the union building and headed back to Memorial bridge, her pain began to subside, being replaced by a pleasant, almost euphoric feeling. Pat was going to make it after all.

1)   Pat's cramps began to increase as she crossed Memorial Bridge. On a biological level, what mechanisms allow the body to differentiate degrees of pain? What does this suggest about the treatment of severe pain?

2)   The cramps, being replaced by a "runner's high," began to subside as she rounded the corner marking his half-way point. What neurological changes might have occurred to cause this "second wind?"

3) Is it possible that it was no coincidence that Pat's second wind occurred as she rounded the corner and recognized it as being the half-way mark? How might the recognition of being half finished reduce feeling of pain?

4) Imagine a drug that doubled the length of the absolute refractory period of all neurons. How might having taken this drug before jogging have affected the experienced described above?

5) It is a well known fact that there is an optimal level of physical exercise for burning calories and that by exercising too rigorously you will actually burn less calories. Use your knowledge of the nervous system to explain this counter productive relationship.

8. Biology Underlying Behavior - Neurons and Neurotransmitters

It was just past 10:00 p.m. when Detective Jaffe received a call to proceed to the home of Dr. Van Mannen...now the late Dr. Van Mannen. When he arrived he was greeted by officers Morling and Wills.

In the reading room, sprawled out in an awkward position in the center of the room, the doctor's body was an unsettling sight.

"It looks like the doctor had a seizure. Of course we can't be sure, but that's what it looks like," offered Wills.

Jaffe's attention was elsewhere. Next to the doctor's body was a broken brandy snifter.

"What do we know about the doctor's mental health as of late," he asked aloud to no one in particular.

"Apparently the doctor has suffered from depression for a number of years," said Morling. "And lately he's been frustrated with forgetfulness. His neighbor tells us that he's been losing his memory, and that it bothered him greatly. Why do you ask, sir? Do you have any ideas?"

"Just one." Jaffe's face began to glow triumphantly. "Did Dr. Van Mannen have...a butler?"

"By God," Wills exclaimed. "He did indeed!"

1) What neurological transmitter(s) are associated with depression? What does this imply about the effectiveness of drug treatments for depression?

2) Dr. Van Mannen's slow memory loss may be due to Alzheimer's disease. What neurotransmitter has been implicated in the onset of this disease?

3)   Jaffe suspects that the butler poisoned his employer. What two poisons might affect neurotransmitters and produce a life-ending seizure? How do these poisons produce their effect?

4)   Which part of the nervous system is responsible for controlling muscles, such as the heart, which were affected by the butler's poison?

5)   The sight of the doctor's contorted body alarmed Jaffe. What physical reactions did he probably experience? Which part of the nervous system is responsible for these changes?

9. Sensation and Perception - Vision

Calvin and Lydia had to drive 45 minutes out of the city to find an isolated field suitable for star gazing. But neither of them were complaining; this promised to be a great evening. Because Calvin and Lydia didn't have many interests in common, finding something they both enjoyed doing wasn't always easy. Star gazing might turn out to be one of them.

Calvin was a real outdoors person and loved camping under the stars. However, his knowledge about what stars, galaxies, nebulae, etc. was pretty limited. On the other hand, Lydia had taken some astronomy at a community college and had a pretty good working knowledge of the names of the constellations as well as the layout of the galaxy.

For the first half hour or so, Lydia pointed out constellations and taught Calvin their names. Then they made up games, such as "who can find the faintest star," and "which star is the brightest". After an hour or so, they decided that they'd had enough for one night. The moon was just rising and looked gigantic as they walked back towards the car.

1)   Calvin and Lydia had to leave the city to star gaze. In psychological terms, what is the excess light of the city called? Why is it harder to see stars in the city?

2)   Would identifying which of two stars is brighter be easier when they were both relatively dim or both relatively bright? Why? What formula is used to predict differential thresholds?

3)   The moon shone off to the left as Lydia and Calvin walked back to the car. At which side of their brain did the message eventually arrive? Outline the optical and neural path by which the image of the moon reached the visual cortex.

4)   Lydia was able to see more faint stars than Calvin. She did this by not looking directly at a star, but off to the side. Why did this trick work? What type of receptor cells are used in peripheral vision?

5)   Lydia tried to teach Calvin to look at a star parafoveally, but he complained that the star off to the side kept disappearing. What is happening?

10. Sensation and Perception - The Senses

"This movie is a real loser," Frank thought to himself. Bad acting, bad directing, bad effects; this movie had it all. During what was intended to be an dramatic rescue scene, Frank decided that he needed to take a break, rose quickly out of his seat, and walked briskly toward the lobby.

Having stood too quickly, Frank was a little dizzy at first, but it passed quickly. Not knowing where he was going exactly, he headed to the mens' room to use the bathroom and wash his hands. Still not wanting to go back yet, he decided to stop at the concession stand and buy some popcorn and a soda. The popcorn, which filled the room with a buttery aroma, was actually a little stale.

Not knowing what else he could do, Frank decided to go head back to his seat. Entering the theater, his eyes adjusted to the darkness quickly and he found his seat.

1)   Why did Frank experience a brief dizziness when he rose to leave the theater? What parts of the body are involved?

2)   What are the four sensations of taste? Which one(s) would respond to eating popcorn? In what area(s) of the tongue are these taste buds located? What does Frank actually mean when he says the popcorn "tastes" stale?

3)   While getting Frank's popcorn, the concession worker burned her hand on the heating element. She grabbed the burned area on her skin and held it very tightly. Why might this help reduce the pain?

4)   How many sensations are mentioned in this story, either explicitly or implicitly? Can you identify more than five? Can you identify more than seven?

5)   How sensitive is the sense of smell? How many different types of receptor cells are involved in the olfactory system? At age 22, is Frank's sense of smell improving or declining?

11. Sensation and Perception - Perceptual Organization

Steph was excited to be going to the annual Spring carnival that came to the campus in mid-May. Besides providing good live music, the carnival boasted a dozen or so smaller side-shows as well as games and even a few rides. The event always reminded her of the state fairs she attended as a child with her father. Picking up a campus newspaper, Steph search for information about this year's carnival.

Among last year's shows that had been Steph's favorite was a young comedian who had performed some very funny ventriloquism. For days afterwards she would remember his act and laugh aloud. Another show she had thoroughly enjoyed was a hologram exhibit. She still was amazed how holograms portrayed images in three dimensions. Hopefully these shows would be here again this year.

Finding the listing of events, Steph was disappointed to discover that the "Sights and Sound" booth had replaced the hologram exhibit with the pointillist paintings of the French impressionist artist Serat.

1)   Using your knowledge of speech reception, can you explain how ventriloquists create the illusion of making a stuffed doll appear to speak? Would a person who has slightly impaired hearing be more or less susceptible to a ventriloquists trick?

2)   How do 3-D movies create the appearance of having a third dimension? Is this the same process that underlies hologram technology? In what ways must the two technologies differ? In what ways must they be the same?

3)   The time that elapsed as Steph read the newspaper article about the carnival was very short. What does this suggest about the feature-analysis approach understanding reading?

4)   Which of the four Gestalt laws of organization can be implicated in the phenomenon that causes pointillist paintings to appear like orderly scenes at a distance?

12. Sensation and Perception - Perception in Everyday Life I

Carol walked around the neighborhood with her two boys, Erik, 11, and Tim, 6. They had three more houses to visit on their annual Halloween trick-or-treating outing. Tim was busy counting up how many chocolate bars he had collected when Erik suddenly cried, "Tim! Look how big the moon is! That means that the werewolves are coming out early this year!"

Tim looked up, wide-eyed. The moon <u>did</u> look huge--and orange, too. "Then I want to go home, now!," he yelled. "I don't want the werewolves to get me!"

"Erik, don't scare your brother," said Carol. "That's just called a harvest moon, Tim. It isn't scary."

Erik turned serious. "How come the moon gets so big sometimes, mom? Is it closer to the earth today?"

Carol explained, "Well, it's really just an illusion. Depth cues--like those trees you see over there--make you think the moon is farther away than it really is. Your brain tries to compensate for this far distance, but since the moon really isn't that far away, your brain ends up making it appear bigger. When the moon is higher in the sky, the depth cues aren't there, so you see the moon at the size you're used to."

1)   As the night goes on, and the moon rises more, the harvest moon disappears and appears to be its normal size again. Explain how you could teach Erik to use his thumb (or some other item) to measure the retinal image of the moon, and prove that it remains the same size as it rises.

2)   Many optical illusions--like the Müller-Lyer illusion--do not work for all people, such as people from non-Western cultures. Why do some illusions not work in these cultures? Do you think all cultures see the harvest moon illusion? Why or why not?

3)   Imagine that we lived on a planet with a moon that was usually low on the horizon. Would the harvest moon effect happen there? On this planet, how would the moon appear to us on a day when it rises high in the sky? Would it appear smaller or larger?

4)   Even though Carol knew why the moon appeared bigger, her eyes were still "fooled" by the harvest moon. What does this say about the level of processing that perceptual processes follow? Can they be interrupted by concentrating very hard?

13. Sensation and Perception - Perception in Everyday Life II

The cry of a nearby infant had awaken Maggie out of her nap. "The gentle rocking motion of the train must have lulled me to sleep," she thought. She rubbed her eyes and peered out the window at the sun rising over a foreign landscape. Maggie was on a long train ride from Seattle to the most northern region of British Columbia, a place with beautiful and unfamiliar scenery.

Still a little tired, she stared absently down at the rocks and flowers that lay close to the train tracks, but the train was going so fast that the blur made her dizzy. Looking up, she noticed a patch of trees on a nearly bare horizon, several miles away. Sooner than she expected, the train approached and passed the little grove. "Wow, those trees weren't so far away!," she exclaimed. "They're just really tiny! I wonder what they're called?" This new countryside was indeed very strange and beautiful.

1)   Why did the objects close to the tracks appeared to be moving faster than objects farther in the distance? What is this phenomenon called? Is it a monocular or a binocular depth perception cue?

2)   What perceptual cues caused Maggie to think the trees were very far away, when they were actually close? What role did her previous knowledge play in her perception of the trees? Would she have made the same mistake if the trees were close to a house, car, or some other familiar object?

3)   When the baby's cry woke her up, Maggie was able to tell that the baby and its mother were to her left rather than to her right. Describe the perceptual process that might have led to this inference.

4)   Although she could have looked out the windows on the opposite side of the train, Maggie focused on the scenery out of her own window. What is this phenomenon called? Do you think Maggie might be able to recall any of the scenery from the other side of the train? Defend your answer.

5)   Compare the ecological theory of perception with the constructive theory of perception. How would the two theories explain Maggie's perception of the small trees?

14. States of Consciousness - Dreams

Juan met his suitemate Mark in line for breakfast at the cafeteria one weekday morning.

"Boy, am I exhausted," Juan moaned. "I felt like I would never get to sleep last night. And then when I finally did, I had the most horrible dream. I was walking home from the library when somebody started to chase me, but I couldn't run because my books were way too heavy. I felt like I was running underwater - it was really frightening. And now this morning I'm feeling so tired!"

"Maybe you can take a nap in class this afternoon to make up for it," Mark joked as he passed the coffee machine, stopping to pour a cup and hand it to Juan, "or at least have a cup of java to make it through the morning."

1)   Did Juan experience a nightmare or a night terror? What is the difference between the two? How often do most people have frightening dreams?

2)   At what stage of sleep did Juan's frightening dream occur? During what part of the night is this stage of sleep most likely?

3) How might Freud interpret Juan's dream? What is the dream's manifest content? What might be the latent content of the dream? To what processes would activation-synthesis theory attribute Juan's dream?

4) How common is the kind of insomnia that Juan experienced? Given what you know about insomnia, how long do you suppose it really took Juan to get to sleep that night?

5) Think about Mark's suggestions to Juan for dealing with his sleepiness. Will they help Juan in the short run? Will they help Juan overcome a chronic insomnia problem? What alternative suggestions would you make to Juan?

15. States of Consciousness - Hypnosis and Mediation

Raindrops began to fall as Lori pulled out of the parking lot and began her long commute home.

"What a way to start the weekend," she muttered, turning on her lights and windshield wipers. But soon she was happily distracted by thoughts about the upcoming weekend. She had been planning a surprise party for her husband Paul for weeks, and as she drove she imagined how excited and pleased he would be when he walked through the door and saw all of his friends. In her mind, Paul's face would light up with surprise, then he would turn to Lori and say, "How did you plan all this without my knowing?"

Lori turned on the radio and found a news hour. She followed the first few stories, but before she knew it she was almost home. She had safely driven almost ten miles, but couldn't remember any of it!

1) How was Lori's daydream about the party different from dreams she may have had at night? In particular, which dreams are more controllable? How does the content differ? How often do most people daydream, on the average? Do you see any important functions of this particular daydream of Lori's? Should Lori be concerned about daydreaming?

2) How would you describe what happened to Lori as she listened to the news? Was she in an altered state of consciousness? Why or why not?

3)   Do you think Lori was in a state of hypnosis? What features does her state have in common with hypnotic states? What features may be different? If you had to guess, what stage of wakefulness or sleep would you say Lori's brain waves resembled during those ten miles?

4)   What features does Lori's experience have in common with meditative states? What features may be different? How does people's memory for meditative states differ from their memory for hypnosis sessions?

16. States of Consciousness - Drugs I

As Lee walked through the student center concourse, an argument among a two students caught his attention. One student was seated behind a table displaying literature and information promoting the legalization of marijuana. Before long, several other students began to participate in the discussion.

"Marijuana is as safe as alcohol. Everyone uses it anyway, so why shouldn't it be legalized," a nearby student was saying.

"But if you legalize it you might as well legalize every other drug too. They're all the same," another student offered.

"But marijuana is not addictive at all. And it has no harmful side effects, either," said another bystander.

"Well, I heard that pot makes you just want stronger and stronger drugs. So if we legalize it, we're just inviting worse trouble."

"Oh, that's silly. It has the same effect as beer. They're practically the same thing," someone from the back shouted.

"I think you all had better get your facts right," said the person behind the table. "Check out these flyers and then we can discuss this issue fairly."

1)   What classification of drug is marijuana? How are its effects different from alcohol? How are they different from narcotics? From stimulants? Which of the classifications of drugs is most addictive?

2)   What makes a drug addictive? What are some major symptoms of drug addiction? How addictive is marijuana?

3)   How common is marijuana use compared to alcohol use? Why do you suppose alcohol is socially accepted, whereas marijuana is largely not?

4)   What is your own opinion about whether marijuana should be legalized. Be sure to defend your opinion with researched based sound evidence and not the faulty arguments given by the students in the story.

17. States of Consciousness - Drugs II

Nikki wasn't sure if she should be worried about her roommate Jodi or not. A lot of times, Nikki found her fun to be with. Jodi was full of confidence and energy, and could stay up all night talking or studying. But other times, she slept all day and acted really depressed, grumpy, and worried. And then there were times when Jodi wasn't in the room at all for days, and she skipped house meetings and classes. Nikki wasn't sure how Jodi was doing in school, but she didn't think she was doing that well. She also suspected Jodi had money problems. Jodi used to ask to borrow money from Nikki occasionally, but now Nikki suspected that she just "borrowed" directly from her purse without asking. Maybe Jodi was just going through a rough time. Then again, maybe it was something more serious.

1)   Which of Jodi's behaviors seems consistent with a drug problem? What common symptoms of drug abuse are missing in this description? Many of Jodi's behaviors could be explained by non-drug-related reasons. Should Nikki be suspicious of a drug problem? What features might help you decide?

2)   Given Jodi's behavior, what classification of drug would you suspect her to be using? Which of her symptoms are common to most drug use?

3)   One possibility is that Jodi is using cocaine. What are the three stages of cocaine withdrawal? What role might classical conditioning play in the third stage of withdrawal?

4)   Jodi's problem might also be related to a heroin addiction. How is heroin addiction most commonly treated? What are the advantages and disadvantages of this treatment? Is there a similar antidote for cocaine addiction?

18. Learning - Classical Conditioning

The phone on the other end of the line rang four times before someone answered. "Hello, Lamar Pet Hospital." Kate recognized the voice as belonging to Pat Berdet, Frisky's veterinarian.

"Hi Pat, this is Kate Holliday. I brought my cat Frisky in yesterday afternoon for some shots." Kate paused to give Pat a chance to think.

"O.K. Sure. I remember now. Frisky hadn't been feeling very well," she said.

"Right, well you told me that Frisky might feel a little sick to her stomach for a few hours, but that if she didn't get over it in 24 hours to give you a call. Well, It's been 26 hours now and she won't eat.

"The funny thing is that she acts like she's hungry. I've been cooking and every time I open a can she comes running, but when I show her that her bowl has food in it, she just sniffs but won't eat it."

Pat thought for a moment, then she seemed to get an idea. "Tell me Kate, did you feed Frisky just before you brought her in to us?"

1) What is Pat's idea about the cause of Frisky's refusal to eat her food, despite showing signs of being hungry? What are the implications of this for classical conditioning theory?

2) Why does Frisky run into the kitchen when she hears a can being opened. What is the conditioned stimulus in this instance? What is the unconditioned stimulus?

3)   Is Frisky's running into the kitchen a conditioned response, an unconditioned response, or both? Explain your answer.

4)   As a kitten, Frisky would sometime run into the kitchen when the electric dicer was turned on. However, she only did this a few times. Explain this behavior in classical conditioning terms.

5)   Kate started Frisky on a dry food diet two years ago, and for the past year Madolyn has not bothered to chase after the sound of a can opener. According to classical conditioning theory, what happened to cause Frisky to stop responding to this sound, and why did she start again?

19. Learning - Operant Conditioning I

Kathy and Brad sat quietly in their bedroom. Brad was reading the letter that Kathy had read half a dozen times since it arrived from the school this morning. The school had written to inform them that their son Jim had been skipping classes again. Apparently the talk the three of them had before the school year began hadn't been very effective. And the timing couldn't have been any worse for Jim. Last weekend, after he borrowed Kathy's car, Jim drove home drunk.

Taking it one problem at a time, Brad and Kathy brainstormed how to deal with these situations. For driving drunk they could take away his driving privileges for a month, or make him spend the next two Saturdays working around the house. For skipping class they could ground him for a week, or offer to increase his allowance if his attendance is perfect for a while. Or they could combine the two punishment; revoke his driving privileges and tell him that they only way to get them back is for perfect attendance.

1) What's the differences between negative reinforcement and positive reinforcement? Give an example of each from the story.

2) What is the difference between a negative punishment and a positive punishment? If Jim was forced to do house work for two weekends, which type of punishment would that be?

3) When is punishment the best choice in dealing with unwanted behaviors? Should either of Jim's behavior problems be handled by the use of punishment?

4) When is reinforcement more effective than punishment in shaping behavior? Why? Should either of Jim's behavior problems be handled by the use of reinforcement?

5) What role do cognitions play in operant conditioning? Consider the effect of forcing Jim to mow the lawn as a punishment if he happens to enjoy moving lawns.

Critical Thinking: General Principles and Case Studies

20. Learning - Operant Conditioning II

As Lucy released the frisbee, her black lab Olivia ran after it. Leaping slightly, Olivia graciously caught the falling frisbee and returned it to the thrower.

"Wow, she's some catcher," mused Lucy's friend Jeff. "How did you teach her to catch like that?"

"Well, I started off by feeding her out of the frisbee so she'd get us to it," Lucy said. Later I'd give her a treat when she chewed on it, then if she caught it when I dropped, and finally she would get the treat only if she chased it down when I threw it.

"Then I had to train her to bring it back, so I started giving her treats every time she returned the frisbee so she got used to dropping it in order to get the reward. I rewarded her only every other time, then less often. Now she gets a treat only once or twice per frisbee game. She's a fully trained frisbee catching machine."

1)   What is the law of effect? Why is not applicable to teaching an animal to do a completely unnatural trick, such as catching a frisbee?

2)   What type of conditioning did Lucy use to teach Olivia to catch a frisbee? What type of reward schedule did she use?

3)   What type of conditioning and reward schedule did Lucy use to teach Olivia to return the frisbee? Why does Olivia continue to catch and return frisbees despite receiving almost no rewards for doing so?

4)   Lucy jokingly calls Olivia a frisbee catching machine. In what way is this analogy appropriate to the principles of operant conditioning?

21. Learning - Observational Conditioning and Overview

The front door of the apartment opened and Tamara heard her father's voice call out. "Is anybody home?" he mockingly asked, knowing that Tamara was eagerly awaiting his return.

"Daddy's home! Daddy's home!," she shrieked.

In one loving motion, Ron swept his daughter up into his arms. While Tammy hugged him tightly, he whispered into her ear, "Where's your mom?"

Tamara responded softly, "She's in your bedroom." Then somewhat louder, "Daddy, you missed my birthday."

"Then I guess it's too late to give you this," he said pulling a play kitchen set out of a bag. Tamara shrieked again. Ron opened the box and started to pull out the play furniture and appliances. Tamara knew just what to do with each new piece.

"I'll cook you a hamburger, Daddy," she said flipping a plastic hamburger with her new toy spatula in her new kitchen. Say, you're a good cook. Did mommy teach you how to cook while I was gone?" Ron said.

Tammy laughed at this joke. He knew that she was not allowed near the stove when it was on.

1)   Tammy proceeded to cook a nine course meal for her father and from that day on the kitchen set was her favorite toy. How would operant conditioning theory explain her love for this toy?

2)   How would classical conditioning theory explain Tammy's attachment to her new toy? Identify the conditioned and unconditioned stimuli and responses.

3)   How would cognitive learning theory explain Tammy's being able to pretend to cook her father a hamburger, despite having never been allowed near a stove while it was on?

4)   How would observational learning theory explain Tammy's ability to "cook" for her father? Identify the four stages of observational learning in this story.

22. Memory - Encoding, Storage, and Retrieval I

Jesse was just returning from her first golf lesson.

"How did it go?" asked her husband, who seemed preoccupied watching his favorite TV news show.

"Fine," she said, laying down her heavy golf bag, "but I noticed something odd about the way the golf pro answered my questions. I thought he would be able to just tell me what to do. Instead, it seemed that in order to remember anything, he would have to act it out himself. Only then could he describe what I was supposed to do."

"That's nice, dear," said her husband, as he stared at a spectacular airplane crash on the TV screen.

Later, when Jesse's husband tried to recall how her lesson had gone, all he could remember was that the golf pro had seemed "odd."

1) What form of long term memory was Jesse showing when she told her husband how the golf pro had acted?

2) The golf pro seemed to have trouble describing how something was done unless he performed the action himself. What form of memory code was he probably relying on?

3)   Jesse seemed surprised by the golf pro's memory process. If the golf pro had been unable to answer her questions immediately, without acting them out first, what kind of memory would he probably have been showing?

4)   Jesse's husband seemed to have trouble remembering what she had said about her lesson because he had not considered it very carefully. Which theory of memory does this explanation most closely resemble?

5)   Which of the 3 memory processes seems to have caused Jesse's husband's memory problem? Why?

23. Memory - Encoding, Storage, and Retrieval II

Mary liked to draw, even during class. From her desk, if she leaned backward and peeked a bit to the left, she could make out the magnificent profile of Johnny Evans, the most popular boy in the school. Then she would try to draw Johnny in the margin of her notebook. She noticed that after each glance, she could almost see his face for a short while, even though she had looked away.

"Mary, you weren't even listening!" said the teacher, awakening Mary from her reverie.

"Yes I was," retorted Mary. "You just asked if anyone could name the nine planets." Actually, Mary had not been listening, but the sound of the teacher's last question had seemed to ring in her ears even so.

"Well, can you name the nine planets?" challenged the teacher.

"No," said Mary, "because they already have names." The class erupted in laughter.

"I know!" pleaded Johnny Evans. "Mercury, Venus, Earth, Mars, Jupiter, Saturn, Uranus, Neptune, and Pluto. I know because the first letters match the sentence `Mary's violet eyes make Johnny stay up nights period.'"

Mary blushed.

1)   Mary seemed to be able to see Johnny's profile "in her mind's eye" for a short time after she looked away.   What form of sensory memory might she have been using?

2)   Later, Mary was also able to remember the sound of the teacher's question, even though she had not been listening. What form of sensory memory might she have been using this time?

3)   What organizational strategy did Johnny use to remember the names of the nine planets?

4)   Johnny was able to combine the names of the planets into a meaningful group of information. What is this kind of grouping called?

5)   Although Mary did not know the names of the planets, she knew for certain that there were nine of them. What type of long term memory did she use to store this information?

24. Memory - Long Term Memory I

June had been nervous ever since she had accepted the invitation from her Aunts, Gilda and Martha, to stop in for tea. Now, late, and frantically looking for their house, June fretted. How was she going to recognize their house when she hadn't been there for fifteen years? All she could remember about the house were some red gardenias on the porch. Unfortunately, it was now the middle of winter. Once again June promised herself to be more careful writing down directions. Suddenly, she saw a house she knew was their's.

Once everyone was settled, tea went well. Aunt Gilda, it seemed, remembered the day Franklin Roosevelt died "as if it were yesterday." She spoke at length, recalling an amazing amount of detail. She and Martha had been together when they had first heard the news.

"It is a wonder," said June, who was genuinely amazed, "that you remember so <u>vividly</u>."

"It is a wonder that you remember so <u>wrong</u>," sputtered Martha, breaking her long silence. "My dear Gilda, I too remember that day as if it were yesterday. Unfortunately, many of your so called details are incorrect!"

1)   Why might June have been able to recall the gardenias, when she forgot everything else about the appearance of the house?

2)   Why might June have been able to recognize the house when she saw it, even though she had not been able to remember what it had looked like?

3)   Both Gilda and Martha had vivid memories of what they were doing when they first heard of Franklin Roosevelt's death. What is the name for this kind of memory?

4)   Apparently Gilda and Martha disagreed on several details of what they were doing when they first heard of Franklin Roosevelt's death. Why might they disagree?

5)   On what kinds of details might Gilda and Martha be especially likely to disagree?

25. Memory - Long Term Memory II

Bob liked to act in his local theater. In a new play, his character, Rex Rains, has been in an automobile accident and suffered complete memory loss for two hours afterward. During those two hours, someone had committed a murder. Despite his memory loss, Rex was a suspect.

In the opening scene, Rex is lying in a hospital bed. The doctor allows Police Inspector Fairway only three questions, because of Rex's delicate condition. Bob's lines in this scene are: "I think, Fairway, she served a strudel," "I can't remember," and "No."

The night before the first performance, Bob fell asleep repeating his lines. He even dreamed about them.

Arriving at the theater opening night, Bob found that the order of his lines had been changed. Then the order was changed again. Confused and worried, Bob mentally associated the order of his lines to a walk through the rooms of his house. Each room he mentally passed through would remind him of the next line.

The scene arrived. Everything went well, until Bob's last line.

"Can you remember," asked Police Inspector Fairway, "what the victim served for dessert that night?"

Bob mentally walked upstairs to his bedroom. "I think, stairway," said Bob, "she served a frudel."

1)   What is the name for Bob's character's kind of memory loss?

2)   Bob originally learned his lines to a degree far beyond what he needed to say them correctly. What is this kind of learning called?

3)   Once having learned the order of his lines, Bob found it difficult to learn a new order. What psychological effect does this resemble?

4)   Opening night, what method did Bob eventually use to relearn the order of his lines?

5)   Even though he had worked very hard, Bob incorrectly recited his lines. Was there anything about the way Bob memorized his lines that might have made the mistake more likely? What other memorization methods could Bob have used?

26. Memory - Forgetting and Improving Memory

Gilda and Martha were sisters. Now, both in their seventies, they found themselves living together once again. And they had started to argue. Today, the issue was whether Gilda, the "prettier" one, had ever been interested in a married man.

"What was his name?" Martha mused, looking out the window. "I am certain I know it." Just then a laundry truck drove by. "Oh! I remember," she cried. "His name was Starch, Robert Starch. I saw that look in your eye, and his marriage wasn't very happy."

Gilda feigned horror. "Why I never! You know that I was blissfully married to Walter for 27 years, and, I never missed church, unlike some people."

"True," said Martha, ignoring the barb. "But this was before you even met Walter. I think you may have forgotten your wilder days. And you must have known that he wasn't happy in the marriage. You yourself told me once that he said that since getting married, life had gone down hill."

"My dear Martha," Gilda chuckled, "he said marriage was like riding a bicycle down hill, meaning that things got easier, not worse."

1)   At first Martha had trouble remembering the "suitor's" name, even though she was sure she knew it. What is the name for this phenomenon?

2)   When Martha saw the laundry truck, she suddenly recalled that the man's name was "Starch." How did the truck jog her memory?

3)   Assume that Gilda had really forgotten her "wilder days." Why might she have been more likely to forget them than her sister?

4)   Martha had the idea that Gilda was interested in Robert Starch. Assuming that this had colored her interpretation of Gilda's facial expression, and memory for what was said, what is the name for this general process?

5)   What process might explain why Martha's memory for something Gilda said might be inferior to Gilda's memory for the same thing?

"Did you know that the back of this chair is broken?" asked Molly.

Penny and Molly were moving Penny's things into their new dorm room. Actually, Molly had been living there for nearly a month, while Penny had been living down the hall. However, early on, Penny realized that her assigned roommate and she were not going to get along well. Fortunately, she was able to convince Molly's roommate to swap rooms with her.

"Yeah, I know. I use it as a nightstand," Penny responded. "A friend of mine was going to throw it out so I grabbed it. Now it's my nightstand"

"No. This is a broken chair," said Molly. "For one thing it's too short to be a nightstand. Plus its got this padded surface and things keep falling off. If this is your nightstand, I can't wait to see what you use as a bed"

"Your wrong, Molly. It works fine. It <u>stands</u> next to my bed, and during the <u>night</u> I can reach things on it. It is therefore a night-stand."

1)   What is deductive reasoning? How does Molly use deductive reasoning to conclude that Penny's chair is not a nightstand? Write out the syllogism that she is using.

2)   How does inductive reasoning differ from deductive? Can you find an example of inductive reasoning in this story?

3)   How do categories affect how people think and reason. How does Penny's and Molly's category for "nightstand" differ? Is the category for desk artificial or natural?

4)   How can heuristics help people make decisions? What type of heuristic does Molly use for deciding what is a nightstand?

Critical Thinking: General Principles and Case Studies

28. Cognition and Language - Problem Solving

Sunday morning was Beth's favorite time of the week. Waking up late, she would walk first to a bagel store and then to the newsstand, both just around the corner. Returning home, Beth would brew a small pot of flavored coffee and spread out on the floor with the Sunday paper, sipping coffee and eating bagels.

Opening up the paper, Beth reflexively turned first to the puzzle page. Beth is very good at the anagram puzzles, but not as good at the "complete the series" puzzles. And then there is a maze for kids to work (which she finds is easier to solve if you start at the end and work backwards).

Finally, there were the mind-teasers. Today's read: Joe has two coins that total 30¢, and one is not a nickel. What are the two coins? After pondering this riddle for a few minutes, it suddenly occurs to her. A quarter and a nickel - "one is not a nickel," but the other is.

1) Describe arrangement problems, transformation problems, and problems of inducing structure. Which of these types of problems does Beth work on in the puzzle pages? Which is she best at?

2) Which of the Sunday puzzles could be classified as an ill-defined problem? Why are these problems so difficult to solve?

3)   How can a means-ends analysis help a person who is trying to solve a maze puzzle? Can this type of analysis sometimes interfere with solving this type of puzzle?

4)   What is the role of insight in solving problems? Are humans the only animals capable of insight? Defend your answer.

Critical Thinking: General Principles and Case Studies

29. Cognition and Language - Problem Solving II

Bill had almost finished reading Agatha Christie's posthumously published "Curtain" and had no idea what to make of it. The incomparable Hercule Poirot, who has been solving criminal mysteries, is very near death. Hastings, his trusted companion, must be the eyes and ears for Poirot, a task that he is not accustomed to. There have been six murders, each of which has been satisfactorily explained by the police. But Poirot believes that the real killer is still at large and vacationing at Styles Court.

Bill gets out a piece of paper and begins writing. Looking at each murder separately, he decides who could have done it. Putting this list together, he is disappointed to find that no one could possibly have committed all six murders. Yet Poirot insists to Hastings that one person has. Suddenly, Bill has a flash of insight. Maybe Hastings, who is narrating the novel, isn't telling the reader everything. Maybe he's hiding something that would tell us that he is the murderer.

1)   What is convergent thinking? How do mystery writers such as Christie utilize convergent thinking to confuse readers?

2)   How does divergent thinking differ from convergent thinking? How does Bill use divergent thinking to arrive at his solution to the mystery?

3)   How can sub-goals be used to solve complex problems? How does Bill use sub-goals to try to solve the mystery?

4)   How do the concepts of functional-fixedness and mental-sets apply to problem solving? Discuss the role of mental sets in Bill's decision to include Hastings as a possible suspect?

5)   It quickly becomes obvious to Bill that his Hastings solution may be wrong. Poirot knows who the murderer is and he doesn't seem to think it's Hastings. However, Bill continues to believe he has solved the mystery. What type of thinking is Bill exhibiting here?

Brad was enjoying his visit home for the winter holidays. Leigh and Tom, his older brother and sister, had also been able to come home for a week, and had brought their own families. Brad was still new at being an uncle, but was having a lot of fun with it. Being an uncle, he found, combined the fun of having kids without any of the obligations.

Joshua was petting Grotto, the family dog, and confided in Brad, "You know what? Yesterday this dog and me played outside and we runned around together."

"Did you have fun when you <u>ran</u> around together?" corrected Brad. To which Josh only nodded.

Joshua's sister, Kelsie, was sitting on the couch just a few yards away and overheard that fun was being had without her. she quickly chimed in, "I want to play dog too." Brad comforted her,

"Tomorrow we can all go outside and play. And," he added, "Grotto knows how to do tricks. She can sit when you tell her, and even fetch sticks if you want."

Both children grinned with excitement.

1) Joshua uses the wrong tense of the verb run. What is this type of mistake called? At what age do children display this type of mistake?

2) Kelsie's speech is also grammatically incorrect. How would psychologists describe the type of speech that she is using? How old would you estimate her to be?

3)   According to learning theory approaches to language, how do language skills develop? What evidence would learning theorists point to in this story to support their case? How do innate mechanisms theories differ from learning theories in explaining language acquisition in children?

4)   How does Grotto know to sit when she is told? Does she understand the English language enough to be able to understand simple commands or is some other mechanism at work?

5)   Grammar deals with what three major components of language? With which aspect is Joshua having difficulty when he uses the wrong form of the verb "run?"

31. Intelligence - Defining Intelligence

Professor Vorwerk quickly handed back the French quizzes that her students had taken two days before. Steve, looking over his test with a smirk that expressed disappointment, turned to Mary. "Hey Mary, how did you do?" he asked.

"Pretty well," she said. "For some reason I do alright on these things. I should have majored in French, I'm getting an A in here and I'll probably fail my engineering course."

"I don't know why I can't get the hang of this class," Steve complained. "I'm thinking of dropping it and trying Spanish next semester. I lived in California for a year so I know a few words already."

"That's right," said Mary. "I forgot that you wrestled there for a year before you came here. Why did you ever leave?"

"I didn't do very well there," Steven said. "Coming out of high school I was used to winning; it was hard getting used to not winning. I guess I just decided that it wasn't worth it. Anyway, it's not like you can turn professional after college."

"Yeah, I guess not." Hearing that Professor Vorwerk had begun to lecture, Mary opened her workbook while Steve searched through his bag for a pen.

1)   How would theories that subscribe to the belief that intelligence is a unitary factor explain Mary's differential performance in her French and engineering course? What contemporary theories can better explain Mary's performance?

2)   Explain the distinction between fluid and crystallized intelligence. Which type of intelligence is Mary using when taking her French vocabulary quizzes?

3)   Describe the concept of emotional intelligence. How would Steve score on a test of this type of intelligence?

4)   What is the distinction between achievement tests and aptitude tests? To which category do intelligence tests belong? To which category do French quizzes belong?

5)   Despite his failing in French, Steve is an excellent athlete. Although traditional tests such as the Stanford-Binet and WAIS would ignore this fact when discussing Steve's intelligence, some contemporary tests would not. Describe one such contemporary test. Do you think that athletic ability should be considered to be a form of "intelligence"? Defend you answer.

32. Intelligence - Variations in Intellectual Ability

Among the budget cuts that the city counsel is considering is a 5% reduction in funds for secondary education. As the principal of one of the junior high schools that could be affected, Karen is worried. Such a reduction would almost certainly mean teacher layoffs and smaller teacher-to-student ratios.

Currently the school offers basic math and English courses for students on three levels: average, below average, and above average. However, a smaller budget may require offering only two levels next year. One possibility Karen is considering is dropping the accelerated courses. After all, the bright kids will do well no matter what. On the other hand, dropping courses designed for below average students would mean that those children would not get the extra attention that they need. No, If push comes to shove, it's the honors programs that will have to go.

1)   What are the levels of mental retardation? Students with which levels can typically attend regular junior and senior high schools?

2)   Many people suffering from mental retardation can trace their condition to biological causes. What is the most common of these biological causes? Can familial retardation be attributed solely to biological factors?

3)   One option that Karen might consider is to integrate slower students into average level courses. What benefits might result from this? Are there any significant drawbacks to this approach?

4)   What fallacy is Karen committing when concluding that accelerated course are relatively unimportant? What are the potential long-term costs to a society that fails to foster gifted students?

33. Intelligence - Individual Differences in Intelligence

With only two positions open, this year's entering graduate class was going to be small. To fill those two position, a search committee had poured over nearly 100 applications to come up with a list of three potential admittances: Melissa Allport, Roberta Guerra, and Don Jackson. A faculty meeting was called to decide which of these three candidates to accept.

Because all three candidates were strong, deciding who to accept and who to reject would be somewhat arbitrary. One suggestion was to accept the two students with the best standardized intelligence test scores. However, another suggestion was to deemphasize intelligence test scores, and instead focus on affirmative action issues in order to increase the number of minorities in the school. Finally, another suggestion was to accept applicants whose parents had attended graduate school, on the theory that they might be better suited for graduate school.

1)   Some psychologists argue that "academic" intelligence -- the kind that is measured by traditional intelligence tests -- is not as predictive of real-world success as "practical" intelligence. What implications might this have for the admittance decision?

2)   The suggestion that applicants whose parents went to graduate school should be admitted seems to assume that intelligence is in part hereditary. Is this belief supported by psychological findings?

3)   Discuss the difference between group differences in intelligence test scores and individual differences in intelligence test scores. Should each be considered in decisions such as the one described in this story? Defend your answer.

4)   Two major explanations for why minority applicants might not score as highly as majority group applicants relate to biases in intelligence tests or the lack of early opportunities. What does each explanation imply about the use of intelligence test scores in graduate school admissions decisions?

34. Motivation and Emotion - Theories of Motivation: Drive, Arousal, and IncentiveTheories

Downtown Pizza was clearly one of the most favored eating places in town. Between six and eight in the evening you could count on having to wait in a line 20 people long. But the line moved fast and the pizza was definitely worth the wait. The lunch rush, however, was considerably less. Taking advantage of this, Susan and Zack meet there frequently for lunch. In fact, Zack was spending so much time and money there this semester that he started working 25 hours (up from 20) a week at a part-time job on campus.

Today, Zack showed up at Downtown at 11 a.m., a solid hour before he was meeting Susan. His goal was to finish a chemistry homework assignment that was due at one that afternoon. He assumed that an hour would be plenty of time. However, at 11:45 Zack still had two fairly complicated problems left. Worried about not finishing in time, he worked diligently, and by ten minutes past noon had finished his assignment. Susan arrived five minutes later.

1) How would instinct theorists explain why people eat? How was this explanation modified by drive-reduction theories? How would incentive theories differ from both of these earlier theories?

2) According to drive-reduction theories, what are primary drives? What are secondary drives? Which drive motivated Zack to add five hours to his work week?

3)   How do arousal theories of motivation differ from drive-reduction theories? What prediction would arousal theory make about the quality of Zack's homework assignment? (Assuming his chemistry homework is a complicated task) Did his performance improve or decline on the last two problems?

4)   How might instinct theory explain why people like Zack and Susan date one another? Contrast this explanation with that offered by drive-reduction theory and arousal theory. In your opinion, which theory provides the best explanation of this phenomenon?

Critical Thinking: General Principles and Case Studies

35. Motivation and Emotion - Theories of Motivation: Opponent-process, Cognitive, and Humanistic Theories

At age 45, Ron Albright is on top of his world. Twenty years ago, after receiving his MBA from Northwestern, Ron borrowed $20,000 from his father to open a small business in Chicago. In ten years he was operating a small chain of 3 stores. Ten years later his company had doubled in size. Last summer Ron sold it for $1.2 million, bought a home in Colorado, and with his wife, Sandi, and their son, Derek, moved West.

Not sure what to do next, the family is devoting this winter to leisure. Sandi is trying to nurture her artistic side by taking pottery and sculpture classes. Ron and Derek are taking ski lessons at a nearby lodge. Their instructor, Judy is very good at her job. She grew up skiing, and still loves doing it. At times, Ron wonders if selling out was the right thing to do. But these doubts grow smaller each day spent here in the mountains with his family.

1)   Most people find downhill skiing to be somewhat frightening the first time they try it. According to opponent-process theory, why would someone ski a second time if it was frightening the first?

2)   How would Maslow's humanistic theory of motivation explain Ron's decision to sell a business that he had worked hard to create? How would cognitive theories explain his decision to sell?

3)   What motivates a person to express one's self creatively through art? At what level of Maslow's hierarchy would artistic motives reside?

4)   According to cognitive theories there are two basic types of emotions. What are they? Which of these motives drove Judy to ski as a child? Which motive lead her to become an instructor?

5)   Judy appears to love skiing as much today as she did growing up. Would this statement surprise a cognitive motivation theorist? Why or why not?

36. Motivation and Emotion - Basic Human Needs: Food and Water

Like many college students, Jenny is currently trying to lose weight. Just losing 10 pounds would put her back to the where she was when she came to college two years ago. So, three weeks ago, she went on a diet for only the second time in her life.

The first time she dieted was in high school. That time had been easy. A simple matter of not eating late, drinking lots of water, and skipping desserts dropped her 10 pounds in just over a month. But this new diet wasn't going as well. All foods looked delicious in the past three weeks. Even the banana dessert served last night looked good - and she hates bananas!

Not only has this diet been harder, but it's also not working. For some reason it now seems impossible for Jenny to lose weight. Every time she weighted herself in the past month, the scale said exactly the same thing - 135. Never closer to 130, never closer to 140. If she had known dieting was going to be this hard, she might never have started.

1)   What is a weight set point? What brain structure is thought to control it? What would happen if this structure were somehow damaged?

2)   Why might Jenny have had a easier time losing weight in high school than in college. Physiologically, what might have changed in between her two attempts to diet that is making it harder this time?

3)   How does our body store unused foods? When a person loses weight, what happens to their fat cells?

4)   Give an example of an external hunger cue and an internal hunger cue. Which is more likely to be effecting Jenny's eating behaviors? Defend your answer.

5)   How would you evaluate Jenny's diet? What types of changes are necessary in order to keep weight off permanently?

37. Motivation and Emotion - Basic Human Needs: Affiliation, Power, and Achievement

Ben and John have been best friends since junior high. In high school they played the same sports (soccer and baseball), took the many of the same electives (Spanish, world history, advanced math, etc), and belonged to the same clubs (Spanish and science). Now in college, Ben and John are roommates in a centrally located low-rise dorm. This evening they are playing darts in the common area.

"Man you are good," said John shaking his head. "I guess it's clear who the better dart player is?"

"Funny thing about darts. You play long enough and you get pretty good at it," joked Ben. "You up for one more game? I'll spot you 50 points."

"Actually, I should take off. I'm going to the Young Democrats meeting in Memorial Hall. It starts in 15 minutes and I want to get there early. But... tell you what. One more game, but no points. `I don't need no stinkin' handicap'" John did his best imitation of popular line from the movie The Treasure of the Sierra Madre.

Ben laughed. "You're on."

1)   What do psychologists mean by the need for affiliation? How would you judge both Ben and John in their level of need for affiliation? What level is typical for college students?

2)   How would you judge both men's need for achievement? Using examples from the story, explain your answer.

3)   How is the fear of failure related to the need for achievement? Which participant is more fearful of losing this final dart game?

4)   Which dart player exhibits characteristics of being high in the need for power? How do men and women who are high in the need for power behave?

5)   Of the four motives discussed above, which seem to be strongly tied to biological drives? Which seem to be more tied to motives that are learned through a culture?

Critical Thinking: General Principles and Case Studies

The changing leaves signaled the return of Autumn to New England. Although Tara had planned to spend this Saturday studying for her humanities midterm, today was just too beautiful to be indoors. Donning her new lined denim jacket and hiking boots (which were a little too tight, but not too painful), Tara started the half-mile walk to a wooded conservation area near campus.

If someone had asked her how she felt as she followed a trail into the woods, it would have been hard for her answer. It was a mix of awe and peacefulness, of inspiration and restlessness. Suddenly, Tara's daydreaming was broken with jump and a start when a three foot milk snake slithered in front of her. Turning around and walking quickly made this particular snake easy to avoid. However, Tara could not shake the fear of running into another snake, and was finally forced to head back to the street -- what a disappointing end to a beautiful afternoon.

1)   Most theories believe that emotions have both a cognitive and a physiological component. Are the two always mixed together or can an emotion be solely one or the other? Consider Tara's fright at seeing a snake and her sense of peacefulness upon entering the woods.

2)   According to the James-Lange theory of emotion, what were the steps that lead to her experiencing of fear the snake? How does this process differ from that proposed by Cannon and Bard?

3)   Tara continued to be frightened even after she successfully avoided the milk snake. How would Schachter and Singer's theory of emotion explain this? In what way does their explanation differ from James and Lange's theory?

4)   Some psychologists attempt to explain emotions in term of the functions they serve. How would a functionalist theory of emotion explain Tara's lingering fear after avoiding the snake? How would it explain the sense of peaceful feelings of being in a beautiful place?

5)   The English language has more than 500 words that describe different colors of emotions. Does this mean that we can experience over 500 different types of emotions? How would evolution theories of emotion such as Plutchik's answer this question? How would Schachter and Singer answer?

39. Motivation and Emotion - Nonverbal Expressions of Emotion

Mark wasn't sure what he wanted to do this evening, so when his friend Lisa called and invited him go see a foreign film, he immediately agreed.

"What's the name of this move were going to see," he asked. Just at that moment a brown Ford coming the other way swerved to make a left turn, forcing Lisa to hit her brakes to avoid a collision.

"Did you see that, Mark?" Lisa's face tightened with anger. "Some people think they're the only car on the road. Anyway,...what was your question?"

"I was asking about this movie you're taking me to. It's in Spanish, right. I hope it's not too hard to follow. Did you ever notice that the emotions in foreign films never seem quite right? Sometimes I find myself wondering what a character is really feeling."

Lisa laughed at Mark's unexpected diatribe on foreign films. "Really, Mark, sometimes I find myself wondering the same thing about you."

1)   Mark is concerned with not being able to understand what emotions the characters in foreign films are experiencing? According to research on facial expressions of emotion, how valid is his concern? Explain your answer.

2)   Some acting techniques stress the importance of actually feeling the emotions that one is acting out. According to the facial feedback hypothesis, is this a difficult task?

3)   How do the facial feedback hypothesis and the vascular theory of emotions differ? How would each explain Lisa's anger at being "cut off" while driving to the movie?

4)   According to the vascular theory, why might laughing make people feel better. In this theory, does laughing precede or follow the experience of positive feelings?

40. Gender and Sexuality - Gender Differences in Behavior

On Wednesdays, the student union offers half-price bowling from 6 to 10 PM. This Wednesday, with school work caught up, Jill and some friends decided to take advantage of this offer. Like Jill, James' family didn't really bowl. On the other hand, bowling was a favorite past-time in both Natalie's and Dan's families.

Arriving at the union building, Dan suggests that they bowl as two teams with Jill and James being on different teams. That way everyone has a chance of winning. He suggests that Jill and he should be a team, because he and James might be unfair - after all, men tend to be better bowlers than women.

Because the union bowling lanes are old there is no computer to keep track of score, so Natalie volunteers to keep score. And just to make the games interesting, James and Dan place a small wager on the game: the loser buys pizza after the game. James later regretted the bet - he and Natalie lost two out of three games and he got stuck with a $20 pizza bill.

1)   Men in the United States gamble much more often than women. Can this fact be explained in terms of observed personality differences between the gender?

2)   Why do you think men tend to be better bowlers than women? Can this be explained by cognitive gender differences? By physiological gender differences?

3)   What gender differences have been traced to hormonal differences? How might hormone based differences affect the outcome of the bowling game?

4)   According to gender schema theory, why might Natalie have volunteered to keep score for everyone?

5)   If asked what they though their chances were of winning the bowling game, would the men and women have given different answers?

41. Gender and Sexuality - Variations of Sexual Behavior

As a school counselor, Melinda attends annual meetings that focus on adolescent concerns. Today she is attending a seminar entitled "Helping Adolescents Cope With The Emergence of Sexuality." The first half of the seminar focused on the troubles of two fictional high-school students, Carol and Ted.

Although she has gone on occasional dates with men, Carol spends most weekends with women friends. Her friendships have always been very close, but lately Carol has noticed a change in her feelings towards some of her friends; feelings of physical attraction have been added to feelings of emotional closeness. These feelings confuse and scare her.

Ted's situation is somewhat different. Still in the throngs of puberty, Ted is frightened by some of the changes he notices in himself. One concern of Ted's is the increasing frequency with which he masturbates. But more than that, Ted is alarmed by the some of the things he finds himself fantasizing during masturbation. Sometimes he imagines aggressive sex, and at other times he imagines watching others have sex. Ted is worried he is losing control.

1)   How common are Ted and Carol's "problems?" What percentage of United States men and women masturbate? What percentage experience at least one homosexual relationship? What percentage are exclusively homosexual?

2)   What are the current trends in attitudes towards sexuality? Will trends be beneficial for people like Ted and Carol?

3)   What causes a person's sexual preferences? Is there any evidence that biological factors predispose one to be either hetero-or homosexual? What role do environmental factors play in theories of sexual preference?

4)   What role to sexual fantasizes play in the people's sex lives? Do Ted's fantasies suggest that he is likely to actually act aggressively during sex?

5)   What advice would you give to both Carol and Ted? Write a paragraph outlining how you would help them cope with their "problems."

42. Gender and Sexuality - Sexual Difficulties and Treatment

After the first part of the "Helping Adolescents Cope With Their Emerging Sexuality" seminar was over a short coffee break was held. During the break, Melinda meet Robert and Celia, who had both help to organize the seminar. Robert had a private practice and specialized in dealing with victims of sexual assaults. He worked primarily with adults, but occasionally with children as well. Celia was a sex therapist who helped adults who were experiencing anxiety or disfunction in relation to their sex lives.

As they talked, the conversation turned to the topic of the upcoming second portion of the seminar, sexually transmitted diseases. Celia's husband was a physician and would be addressing the seminar. For the last five years he had been working with AIDS patients all over the world. Recently he had been to Thailand, where the incidences of AIDS are very high. Today he was going to share some of his experiences, emphasizing what could happen in the United States if something isn't done to educate people about sexually transmitted diseases.

1)   As a sex therapist, what kinds of problems is Celia likely to encounter? Will she work more with men or with women?

2)   In the US, what groups are most at risk for contacting the AIDS virus? Are these the same groups that are at risk in other world regions?

3)   How common is child sexual abuse? Give a brief profile of the average sex offender. At what age are children most at risk for being sexually assaulted?

4)   Compared to victims of other violent crimes, how severely are rape victims affected by their trauma? Can you explain this? In what ways do psychologists explain the rapist's behavior?

5)   Why is it important for women as well as men to change their attitudes about date rape? What types of ambiguity exists that put a woman in danger of being forced to have intercourse?

43. Development: The Beginnings of Life - Basic Issues in Developmental Research

Jane Elizabeth, a fifth grade teacher at the Spruce Elementary School, was among the first to notice vice principal Kay's puzzling new behavior. It began with Kay giving up smoking and drinking after 20 years. But when the book "The First Trimester" was found on Kay's desk, the puzzle was solved. Shortly thereafter, Kay took maternity leave.

Much to her surprise, Jane found herself promoted to acting vice principal.

"This could be my big chance," she thought. Jane saw herself as the right person in the right position. All she needed was the right crusade. Making her usual walking tour around the building, she wondered what this crusade could be.

As she walked past a display of essays written by fourth and fifth graders, it dawned on her. Why were the fifth graders' essays so much better the fourth graders? Were the fourth grade teachers getting lax?

Needing more evidence before she "took corrective action," Jane mandated a vocabulary test of the fourth and fifth grades. The fifth graders clearly performed better, further supporting her idea that the fourth grade teachers needed attention.

1) What problem was Kay probably trying to avoid by not drinking alcohol while she was pregnant? Why did she give up smoking? Is there a period during which these concerns are especially important?

2) Using a technique called ultra-sound, Kay was able to see a picture of her unborn baby at 10 weeks. What features would be prominent in the ultra-sound? What stage of development is her baby in at this time?

3) What type of research was Jane's vocabulary test? What are the advantages and disadvantages of this type of research? Can you think of another explanation for the results of her study?

4) Suppose that instead of testing the fourth and fifth graders at the same time, Elizabeth had tested the same students, first while they were in the fourth grade, and later while they were in the fifth grade. What type of study would this be? Would she have found different results?

Critical Thinking: General Principles and Case Studies

44. Development: The Beginnings of Life - Early Effects on Personality

After his sizable Thanksgiving dinner, Ted lay down, reclining across the living room rug. It was time for the family's annual post Thanksgiving dinner discussion of family history. As always, the conversation quickly turned to Ted and his identical twin brother, Stan.

"Mom practiced piano almost every day while she was pregnant with Stan and me," Ted said to the ceiling. "That explains our talent for Chopin."

"Don't get me wrong," his sister Alissa interrupted, "but I always thought the prenatal music lessons were hogwash. Seems to me, talent is inherited, just like personality."

"Well, then Stan and I sure inherited different personalities," said Ted. "For example, where is he now? I can't believe that his social calendar was so full that he forget his family."

"He always was outgoing," observed Alissa. "Just like you were always shy."

"Actually," replied Ted, "Stan realized he actually <u>liked</u> all that attention in third grade. The teacher forced him to play Abraham Lincoln in the school play, just because he was tall." Ted's voice dampened slightly. "I was out with the flu."

1)   Stan thought his mother had introduced him to the music of Chopin before he was born. What scientific evidence, if any, suggests that such prenatal learning is possible?

2)   Ted and Stan differed in their level of shyness. Considering that they are twins, do you find this surprising? Defend your answer. Is there any evidence to support Alissa's contention that shyness is inherited?

3)   To what are psychologist referring when they speak of the "nature-nurture issue"? How does maturation relate to this debate? On what side of the nature-nurture issue would an interactionist fall?

4)   Why is the nature-nurture issue important? What are its roots? Where do most psychologists stand on this issue today?

5)   List three physical, three intellectual, and three emotional characteristics that are heavily influenced by genetics. List some characteristics that are less influenced by genetics.

45. Development: The Beginnings of Life - Social Development

Every Friday, Emmitt and Lauren sat down and worked out weekend responsibilities. As the parents of two daughters and one son, there were enough responsibilities to go around. After agreeing that Lauren would help the kids with their homework tomorrow morning, and that Emmitt would take them to soccer practice tomorrow afternoon, they turned whether or not to allow Sara to spend the night at her friend Julie's house tomorrow night even though she was supposed to be grounded for not cleaning her room.

As usual, Emmitt pleaded Sara's case. Lauren had always accused him of letting Sara walk all over him. He doted on her right from the start, taking charge of all aspects of her upbringing. He even convinced Lauren not to breast-feed, wanting to help bottle-feed Sara himself in order to build that special bond usually reserved for mothers and children.

"Emmitt, it's for her own good. Children need to know what limitations and rules are, and that actions have consequences. The best environment for child rearing is where they know exactly what is expected, and that any deviation will be punished. We can't let her go to the sleepover."

1)   Among what three types of patenting styles do psychologists distinguish? How would you describe Emmitt's and Lauren's patenting style? Defend your answer.

2)   In general, Emmitt is in charge of setting and enforcing rules for Sara and Lauren is in charge of Sara's sister and brother. In what ways would Sara and her siblings differ as a result of different parenting styles?

3)   Define the concept "attachment" as it is used by psychologists to describe parent-infant relationships. What types of attachment do psychologists distinguish?

4)   What is the role of breast-feeding in the development of attachment? Was Emmitt correct in thinking that the type of attachment brought on by breast-feeding is unique?

5)   What roles do fathers traditionally play in raising children? How are these roles changing? Consider how Lauren and Emmitt are dividing time with their children on Saturday. Is this typical of most families today? Why or why not?

46. Development: The Beginnings of Life - Cognitive Development

"Daddy, can I have two apples in my lunch tomorrow?" asked 10 year old Myia. Myia, with her father and little sister Lydia, had spent the better part of a chilly October morning picking apples at Bartlett Farms.

"Honey, with all the apples we picked today, you can have as many apples as you want in your lunch. But first, you have to help me cut and peel these apples here for the applesauce."

"I'm going to eat three apples!" shouted Lydia.

As they waited for the apples to cook, the three played games in the living room. However, after a long morning, the girls were both irritable. When they played hide and seek, they argued over where to hide. When they played with crayons, they fought over the colors.

Four hours later the apples were cooked and mashed into sauce. Myia and Lydia watched excitedly as their father poured applesauce from the big bowl into the smaller storage bowls. As they watched their father, the girls divided up the bowls between themselves. Surprisingly, there was almost no arguing over which bowls belonged to whom.

1)   According to Piaget, through what four stages of cognitive development do children progress? At what ages does this typically occur? At age 10, in which stage is Myia most likely to be?

2)   Lydia is not very good at hide and seek. Often she will throw a blanket over her to hide but not realize that her leg or half her body is uncovered. How would Piaget's theory explain this? At what stage of cognitive development is she?

3)	When choosing which containers of applesauce they wanted, Myia tended to pick short fat bowls, while Lydia picked tall skinny bowls that didn't hold as much. Assuming that they both love applesauce, why did the girls tend to chose these different types of bowls?

4)	According to Piaget's theory, children progress through distinct stages of cognitive development. How has this stage-view been questioned? Do children simple wake up one morning understanding principles of conservation that were confusing before?

Walking through the doors of Lanier High for the first time in five years was a strange feeling for Chuck. It seemed like only a few months ago he and his friends had roamed these halls like they owned them. In a way it still felt like that, like the halls had been waiting for him to return. Well, here he was. The newest math teacher at Lanier High.

Chuck's sense that times had stood still at Lanier shattered after his first day. Time at Lanier hadn't stood still, it had accelerated. These kids were a whole new generation of student. Not only did they look as if they should still be in junior high (was he that small in high school?), but they acted like it as well. They seemed to have no sense of what was appropriate and what wasn't, of what was right and wrong. When a particular student gave him grief during lunch, Chuck actually caught himself taking comfort in the fact that, like all adolescents, this kid was probably going through some very rough times. Chuck is quickly developing a feeling that, unlike each of the past five years, this year was going to be a long one.

1)   In the morning, Chuck teaches a freshman course made up of 14-year-olds. What are the major physical developments that these students are going through?

2)   According to Kohlberg's theory of moral reasoning, at what stage are most of Chuck's students? Are Chuck and his students at different stages? Defend your answer.

3)   During adolescence, what does Eriksonian psychosocial theory say is these students' biggest social task? What would constitute a successful resolution of this task? What would constitute an unsuccessful resolution?

4)   As a young adult, what does Eriksonian theory view as Chuck's primary social task? Describe a successful and an unsuccessful resolution of this task.

5)   Is Chuck correct in assuming that for most people adolescence is a difficult time? What are the major problems experienced by teenagers today? How have these problems changed over the years?

Christine and Jeff have been dating for seven years, but surprisingly are not married yet. Meeting in the fall of their second year at college, they dated steadily for the last two and a half years. After graduation, they moved in together. Christine put her finance degree to work at an accounting firm, and Jeff began taking graduate courses in the school of education.

Because they wanted to get their careers in order before getting married, they decided to wait until Jeff completed graduate school. However, these plans had to be changed when Christine decided that she wanted to go back to school to get her MBA. So, after two years of being the bread-winner, Christine and Jeff switched roles; now he was the bread-winner and she the student.

This May Christine will have her MBA. Their financial future heading in the right direction (she has already received several impressive offers), Christine and Jeff can wait no longer to be married. Arrangements are being made for a June ceremony.

1) In what ways is Christine and Jeff's relationship characteristic of the 1990s? In what ways was their parents dating history likely to be different?

2) Christine, more than Jeff, wants to have children soon. What biological factors make having children sooner less complicated than later? Can men or women have children later in life?

3)   At what age does physical strength and reflexes reach their peak? At age 26, are Christine and Jeff's physical abilities increasing or decreasing?

4)   How do most husbands and wives divide household chores today? Does this trend differ for couples such as Christine and Jeff in which the woman is the primary provider?

5)   Christine is confident their marriage will stand the test of time. Statistically, what are the odds that this marriage will end in divorce? What are the chances that Christine will raise a child as a single parent?

49. Development: Adolescence and Adulthood - Late Adulthood

Nine-year-old Jenny handed the joystick to her grandmother, Rose. "Your turn, Grandma Rose. I got up to the fourth level, so I'm just about to beat you!" The two were playing video games; it was a regular pastime on the days that Rose babysat for Jenny.

"Well you'd better watch out, because I'm about to beat my high score. I'm having a good day today!"

Just as the game ended, Jenny's father came home from work. "Who won today?" he asked, grabbing Jenny in a big hug.

"Grandma did. Again. Maybe when I'm a little older I'll be able to beat her. Can Grandma stay for dinner?" Jenny asked her father.

"Sorry sweetheart, but I've got to run. I've got to go to a city council meeting, and afterwards I'm meeting some of the girls for dessert. Maybe next week I'll be able to stay." Rose pushed herself out of the chair in front of the video monitor and began to get her coat.

"I'm going to practice nonstop until then!" Jenny challenged.

1)   Think about the kinds of motor skills it takes to play a video game well. As they both get older, who do you suppose will get better at the game, Jenny, Rose, or both? Support your answer.

2)   How do older adults acquire new skills? Would Rose's video game ability depend on crystallized intelligence or fluid intelligence? Describe how the two kinds of intelligence change as adults get older.

3)   Rose seems to lead a pretty active life. What does research say about older adults like her? Does her lifestyle seem more in line with the disengagement theory of aging or the activity theory of aging?

4)   Rose is likely to forgets appointments unless she writes them down on a calendar. Is Rose's forgetfulness typical of older adults? What types of memory loss (i.e., short-term, long-term, semantic, or implicit) are most common in old age? What types are not vulnerable to aging?

50. Personality - Freudian Theory: Psychosexual Development

Kara and her twin brother Chris just turned five. For their birthday their parents, Carroll and Kathy, are taking them to a favorite dinner place - a pizza restaurant filled with games for kids, including an enclosed area two feet deep in plastic balls where they can jump around. When they get to the restaurant, Kara grabs her father's hand and pulls him towards the door. Chris does the same with his mother.

Although Kara and Chris are twins, their behavior at the restaurant could not have been more different. As always, Kara is neat and polite; watching out for younger children as she plays. Chris, on the other hand, yells and makes lots of noise and tends to be messy. One of his favorite game here is the plastic swords and he runs around pretending to cut off other children's arms and legs. Kara also enjoys playing with swords, put is not nearly as aggressive with them.

1)   What significance would Freud see in the children's wanting to hold their opposite-sex parent's hand while crossing the parking lot? What might this signify about their stage of psycho-sexual development?

2)   According to Freudian theory, why might Chris be such a loud boy? What stage of development is associated with this type of behavior? Can you think of any other explanation for this type of behavior?

3)   At what psycho-sexual stage do children go through toilet-training? If Freud met these two children, what would he conclude about each of their experiences with toilet-training?

4)   How might Freud interpret the twin's behavior with the play swords (assuming the sword represents a phallic symbol to the children)?

5)   The twins' parents believe they spoiled them the first two years. Every cry was immediately attended to and some offering, usually milk or food, was made. What would Freud predict about the consequences of this on their adult personalities?

51. Personality - Freudian Theory: Defense Mechanisms

Laura is having a bad week. The first of her final exams is tomorrow and the pressure is really on her this time. Her parents were not at all happy about her grades last term and threatened to take her car away if she didn't improve her grades this term. Although she is doing well so far, next week's finals could make or break her grade point average for the semester.

As she sits in the library, her worry turns to anger.

"Where do they get off threatening me," she thinks to herself. "I should fail all my finals, that would show them."

Now, too upset to concentrate, Laura decides to go for a jog to let off steam. There will be time to study tomorrow morning before the exam, and although her friend Jenny, who took the class last semester, told her the final will be tough, Laura doesn't believe her. How could the final for a 100 level course be that hard? Besides, Jenny was probably nervous about having to get a good grade and choked under the pressure. She can be so stupid.

1)   Explain the Freudian defense mechanism displacement. Is there any evidence in this story of Laura using this mechanism? Consider her thoughts about both Jenny and about her parents.

2)   When she got too upset to study, Laura decided to go jogging. This is an example of what type of defence mechanism? Did Freud consider this to be healthy behavior?

3)   What is projection. What behavior of Laura's could be viewed as projection. What does this behavior tell us about how Laura really feels about her upcoming test?

4)   Failing a test to make a point seems a very childish thing to do. How would Freudian theory view this behavior? What name did Freud give it?

5)   A common method for coping with stress is through denial. How does Laura use denial to reduce her own level of stress? What are the costs and benefits of this strategy?

52. Personality - Trait, Humanistic, and Learning Theories

"Kate! Wait up. Where 'ya headed?" yelled Deborah, to her friend, Kate as she was leaving the library.

"I have to be at work in 30 minutes," Kate told her.

"Aahh, the record store. How is life in the record business anyway? By the way, did a guy named Paul start working there," Deb queried.

"Yeah, he did," said Kate. "Do you know him? He's a pretty nice guy. And he's fun to work with, he cracks jokes and does funny stuff."

"Really? Are we talking about the same Paul, Paul Darden?" asked Deborah. "Paul's usually pretty quiet and shy. I mean he's nice, but just not very friendly."

"Well I've only worked with him a couple of times, but he's not shy at work. He's the first one to talk to customers who come in. Plus he know a lot about music. He has an amazing memory. People are always surprised when he knows the group who recorded some song they like, but can't recall the name."

"I don't know," puzzled Deb. "That sure doesn't sound like the Paul Darden I know."

1)   How would trait theories of personality evaluate Paul? How would these theories deal with the differences in his behavior in different situations?

2)   How would learning theories of personality account for the variation in Paul's behavior in different situations? How does this approach differ from trait theory approaches?

3)   According to humanistic theories of personality, why might Paul be outgoing and confident sometimes, and shy at other times? According to humanistic theory, which woman has seen the "real" Paul, Kate or Deb?

4)   Compare how each of these theories treat situational factors when describing Paul's personality. Which theory or theories believe that situations can control people's behavior? Do these theories view situational control over behavior as a positive or negative thing?

5)   How sociable is Paul? Discuss this question from a trait, learning, and humanistic viewpoint.

53. Personality - Integrity Tests, Intelligence Tests, and Race Norming

During the last week of May, Stiegelman's departments store conducts interviews to fill summer positions. Each summer they hire between 10 and 20 workers from a pool of more than 50 applicants. Cheryl, who as an African-American woman is used to being in the minority, hopes to be one of the 20 who find work, and not one of the 30 who don't.

In the first phase of the interview process, Stiegelman's asks applicants to fill out two personality questionnaires: an intelligence test, and an integrity test. Recognizing the integrity test, Cheryl has a pretty good idea what the "correct" answer to each of the questions is and quickly fills this form out first. Moving on to the intelligence test, Cheryl realizes that finding the correct answers on this questionnaire will be more difficult. Knowing that these tests frequently are culturally biased in favor of the dominant culture, Cheryl cannot help but wonder whether this test is a fair assessment of her abilities.

1) When Cheryl asked a Stiegelman's manager whether this intelligence test was valid, he told her that the test had a high test/retest validity. This means that people who take the test twice generally score about the same each time. Is this an adequate answer to Cheryl's question? Explain your answer.

2) How might Steigelman's compensate for any cultural biases of their intelligence tests? Imagine that of the 50 applicants, only four are African-American. How will this complicate Steigelman's attempts to compensate for cultural biases?

3)   A problem with many self-report tests is that people can lie on them (even on integrity tests). Describe two personality-assessment methods that overcome this problem? Do these methods have drawbacks?

4)   How would trait, humanistic, and behavior theories of personality view integrity tests? Which theory would be most supportive of their use?

54. Health Psychology - Stress and Coping I

While most doctors her age seem to be accustomed to working under such stressful conditions, Colleen feels that she may be growing less able to cope with the pressure. During one month, while working in the emergency rooms at Emerson County Hospital, Colleen treated more gunshot wounds than in six years working for the United States army.

Now on her way home from a particularly exhausting day, Colleen would normally think about her husband Scott and daughter Kim waiting at home for her. But tonight she'll be coming home to an empty house; Scott and Kim are spending the weekend at a father-daughter camping retreat.

Despite being physically exhausted, it would be difficult for her to fall asleep until she was able to unwind from the tensions of the day. On days like this Scott was able to help by massaging her muscles while she described the events of her day. Without that backrub, Colleen knew that it was going to be a couple of hours until she could get any sleep.

1) Why does Colleen find relief from her stress in backrubs? In what way might this help her?

2) After stressful days, Scott can be a great source of comfort for Colleen. In what ways does having social support help people deal with stress?

3) What are the three categories of stressors? Which types has Colleen experienced recently?

4) When Colleen does manage to fall asleep, it is a restless sleep. In her dreams she once again relives an experience that occurred during the Persian Gulf War three years ago, when a scud missile exploded less than 50 yards from her quarters. Describe the phenomenon that Colleen is experiencing.

5) Although many war veterans experience problems such as Colleen's, many more don't. Discuss this in terms of the "psychological" nature of stress. What difficulties does this pose for stress-theorists that assign fixed stress values to events when determining a person's level of stress?

55. Health Psychology - Stress and Coping II

Now mid-way through her finals-week, Laura is exhausted. This morning she woke up at 6:30 to study for a morning exam, skipping breakfast and disrupting her sleep schedule. Returning from her exam, Laura passed out on the couch, waking up an hour later feeling only slightly more rested. Half asleep, Laura put on an exercise outfit and jogging shoes. "By the end of this week," she mumbles, "I'll have run 100 miles."

The jogging helps. Returning home she feels more awake and less stressed about the test (despite her last minute efforts this morning the test went badly). Feeling hungry for the first time in since yesterday afternoon is a good sign. But what to do after a late lunch? Although her chemistry exam is scheduled for tomorrow, the idea of studying was not appealing; it didn't help this morning why should help tomorrow. Instead, Laura headed out to rent a movie, something funny to take her mind off tests.

1)   Efforts to cope with stress can be either emotion-focused or problem-focused. Explain this distinction, using illustrations from Laura's behavior.

2)   At what stage of Selye's General Adaptation Syndrome model is Laura? During this story, has her stress changed stages? Explain.

3)   Can Laura's recent loss of appetite be attributed to stress? What does it mean to say that an illness is psychosomatic?

4)   Laura felt much better after jogging. In what ways does exercise help reduce levels of stress?

5)   How can stress lead to learned helplessness? Some psychologists might say that Laura's renting a movie is a sign of learned helplessness, while other might say that she is using a stress-reduction tactic. How would you explain her behavior?

56. Health Psychology - Psychological Aspects of Health I

In recent years, medical knowledge and technologies have grown tremendously. As a consequence, more people today live longer with conditions they know may ultimately be fatal. Unfortunately, living with a potentially terminal disease can be very difficult psychologically. In response to this, a number support groups have sprung up to offer counseling for the terminally ill. The groups not only improve psychological functioning, but have actually improved the prognosis of many forms of cancer and other diseases.

Also in recent years, doctors have begun to notice a surprising similarity among patients suffering various heart ailments. These patients tended to be highly ambitious, competitive, and preoccupied with deadlines. This personality trait is now know as Type A personality type, and over the past 20 much literature and research supports it's association with increased incidents of heart disease.

What do these two findings have in common? They demonstrate that psychological health is important for physiological health, and that understanding emotions and attitudes is important for medical doctors as well as psychologists.

1)   What type of attitude is associated with increased cancer survival rates? How do survival rates of people who deny they have cancer at all compare to those of people who accept that they have cancer, but not that it will kill them?

2)   John reports being extremely self-confident and very happy with his life. What is the association between this pattern and heart disease? Between this pattern and surviving cancer? Explain your answers.

3) Philosophers have long believed the mind and the body to be distinct and discrete entities. How do psychologists explain that mental processes can affect physiological ones in general, and can physiological health specifically?

4) Type As are more likely to suffer a heart attack than Type Bs (people who are not Type As). Does this mean that being a Type A increases your chance of having a heart attack?

5) Some psychologists believe that being a Type A does not promote heart disease, but rather being a Type B helps prevent it. Discuss the merits of this argument. Consider that 100 years ago heart disease was relatively rare and today it accounts for 1 in 3 deaths in our society.

57. Health Psychology - Psychological Aspects of Health II

Martha started smoking her freshman year of high school. It was not something she took to right away, but rather smoked only with her friends in the beginning. In those early days the best thing about smoking were the rituals, such as tapping the package to pack the tobacco and lighting another person's cigarette.

In time Martha grew more and more comfortable with her new habit, and by her junior year she averaged two or three packs a week. But even then she smoked primarily on weekends. It wasn't until her senior year that she smoked alone and at home with any frequency. That's when her parents found out about her smoking.

Although smokers themselves, they pleaded with her to quit, saying that they would quit if they could. In fact, both her mother and father had, on separate occasions, tried unsuccessfully to stop. Both were furious that their daughter had adopted their habit.

1) In the preparation stage, future smokers develop ideas about the role of smoking in their culture. Where might Martha have developed these ideas?

2) At what point does the initiation period end and the period of being a smoker begin? What important psychological event occurs causing this transition?

3)   Smoking is both psychologically and physiologically addictive. Discuss how both addictions might have caused Martha's parents' attempts to stop smoking to fail.

4)   What role to rituals play in the formation and continuation of smoking?

5)   Nicotine is physically addictive. Some psychologists now think that nicotine can become emotionally addictive as well. Describe this process and how it works.

58. Health Psychology - Physician-Patient Relationship

"Hi John, how are things this morning," asked Dr. Anderson sliding closing the cloth curtain that sectioned off the examination room.

"Just fine, Dr. Anderson. How's my cholesterol?" asked John who suffered from an inherited condition that raised his blood cholesterol levels.

"Well, it's not as low as I expected," said Dr. Anderson. "You have been taking your medication, haven't you?"

"Yea. I hardly ever forget," he lied. Actually, John had a hard time getting used to taking medications and forgot to as often as not.

"Well," Dr. Anderson continued, "how about your diet. Have you been eating foods high in saturated fats and cholesterol? And are you doing aerobic exercises?"

"Yeah, I work out still. And I <u>think</u> I'm avoiding fats."

"That's a good guy. Don't want to eat nasty fats," mumbled the doctor to himself as he scribbled down John's answers, not hearing John's slight emphasis on the word "think".

Finishing his writing he rose to leave. "Well, John, keep up the good work and we'll see you in six months."

1)   John lied about how often he forgets to take his medication. How might Dr. Anderson's behavior have made John want to lie? What aspects of patient-physician relationships might make patients lie to their doctors?

2)   How is communication between patients and physicians complicated by language? Is there any evidence that the level of language used by Dr. Anderson is difficult for John to understand? Defend your answer with examples.

3)   Dr. Anderson's language becomes child-like near the end of his interview, referring to fats as "nasty." How does this affect the patient-physician relationship?

4)   Imagine that you are to speak to incoming freshman how to get the most out of their health-care providers. What information would you give them?

5)   Some people don't trust doctors or hospitals and are not likely to follow medical advise. What responsibilities does a physician have to these people? Describe some suggestions for how these might be fulfilled?

59. Abnormal Behavior - Defining Abnormality

A graduate student in the school of engineering, Martin is motivated, intelligent, and respected by the faculty and fellow students. Because he is generally extremely competent, Martin's friends are often surprised to discover that he can be quite fearful under common circumstances. For instance, during thunderstorms he becomes exceedingly anxious in general, and particularly fearful of any electrical device, including hand-held calculators.

Martin is also extremely afraid of airplanes and has never flown in one. When attending a conference on the West coast last year, traveling by train cost him an extra two days of travel time. Furthermore, an upcoming international conferences being held in Spain seems out of the question. But perhaps most perplexing is his superstitious fear of the number 13. He refuses to live or work on the 13th floor of a building. Although Martin is aware that his fears are somewhat irrational, he has no desire to change himself. After all, no one is perfect.

1)   Many become somewhat anxious during thunderstorms and many people are afraid of flying. However, the level of Martin's anxiety during these events is uncommon. Using the deviation-from-the-average definition of abnormality, discuss his fear of flying and of thunderstorms.

2)   A fear of the number 13 has considerable precedence in Western society. How would this fear be viewed according to the deviation-from-the-ideal definition of abnormality?

3) How would the abnormality-as-a-sense-of-subjective-discomfort approach view Martin's phobias? Be sure to distinguish between the immediate discomfort he feels in the presence of feared objects and the absence of discomfort when he reflects on his somewhat irrational fears.

4) Although Martin's fears are costly in terms of travel time and missed opportunities, overall his life is a successful one. How would the abnormality-as-inability-to-function approach view Martin's condition?

5) After considering Martin's fear in light of each of the four approaches to defining abnormality discussed above, what conclusion would you offer about the "normality" of Martin's behavior? Which definition(s) do you consider most relevant in this case?

60. Abnormal Behavior - Models of Understanding Abnormality

When her alarm clock sounded at 7:00 a.m., Kim groggily reached over to hit the snooze-bar. Cracking her eyes open just enough to see her clock, she was suddenly startled by the image of a strange woman crouching at the side of her bed. Frightened, Kim tried to scream but found that she couldn't. Then, as suddenly as the vision had appeared, it disappeared.

These morning frights were becoming more and more common for Kim. After a dozen or so scares, she decided to visit a neighborhood counselor, who advertised "free initial consultations." While discussing these experiences with the counselor, Kim was confused when the conversation turned to the history of the house in which she lived. When she inquired about the tangent they had taken, her counselor explained that he believed that Kim was completely psychologically healthy. The visions, he explained, were probably spirits visiting her from the afterlife. Kim left quickly, surprised at the counselor's bizarre explanation.

1) Are Kim's visions a sign of abnormality? Which approaches to defining abnormality would view them as abnormal? Which would not? Describe and defend your own opinion of her case.

2) What model of abnormality is Kim's counselor using in his diagnosis? What treatment, if any, would he prescribe?

3) Kim's, unsatisfied with her original counselor, went to two additional ones. One diagnosed her as suffering from a form of hallucination that affects people when they awaken from a dream and images of the dream linger into the wakened state. Which model of abnormality does this explanation appeal to? What type of treatment might this colleague suggest?

4) The third counselor suggested that Kim was probably seeing visions of people from her childhood, a sign that Kim is repressing some traumatic memory. He is fearful that these intrusive visions will become more severe over time. Identify the model of abnormality that this explanation appeals to and the type of treatment is might suggest.

5) Briefly consider the behavioral and humanistic models of abnormality. What would each suggest about the roots of Kim's visions?

61. Abnormal Behavior - Anxiety Disorders

Paul has always been what his parents described as "a fearful person." Easily and exaggeratedly upset by minor incidents, he was called a "cry-baby" in grade school, a "sissy" in high school, and "over-emotional" by college peers. Even when things are going well in life, Paul complains of being unable to relax, and reports being fearful of losing control of his things.

Although Paul has had these difficulties for as long as he can remember, he was able to deal with them in college. Because he attended a college in his hometown, his family and social network remained in place and helped him cope during these years. However, a tough job market lead to his taking a job out of state, and his condition worsened. Although his parents have recently encouraged him to speak to a doctor or counselor about his problem, he has resisted their efforts.

"After all," he tells himself, "I am not crazy."

1)   How would the most recent revision of the DSM diagnose Paul's condition? To what general type of disorder does this diagnosis belong? What other diagnoses fall under this class of disorders and how do they differ from Paul's?

2)   Paul's younger brother suffers from the same types of symptoms. How would the medical model of abnormal behavior explain this fact? How would the socio-cultural model? How would the psychoanalytic model?

3)   In what sense is Paul's behavior abnormal? Which definitions of abnormality would classify his condition as "abnormal?"

4)   Paul is reluctant to get professional help in part because of the stigma of being classified as having a psychological disorder. Discuss this aspect of the classification approach to understanding and treating abnormal behavior. Are there any alternatives that would involve less of a stigma for sufferers?

62. Abnormal Behavior - Somatoform Disorders

Yvette had played volleyball ever since she was a child. Her mother had been a standout player in college, and Yvette was set to follow in her footsteps, earning a scholarship to the same college at which her mother had won respect 30 years earlier.

Although excited about her situation, Yvette also experienced anxiety over the prospect of not living up to her mother's expectations. As the season grew nearer, her anxiety grew more acute. Then, while practicing services a week before their first match, Yvette suddenly noticed that she had no feeling in her hand. The numbness persisted despite medical reports finding no evidence of any neurological or other physical problems. It looked like Yvette was going to miss the first match of her college career and possibly more; the team doctors would not allow her to play while the numbness persisted.

1)   How would the most recent revision of the DSM diagnose Yvette's condition? To what general type of disorder does this diagnosis belong? What other diagnoses fall under this class of disorders and how do they differ from Yvette's?

2)   How might the psychoanalytic model of abnormal behavior explain Yvette's particular type of paralysis? How might the medical model? How might the humanistic and cognitive models?

3)   Image that you are a therapist and are aware of Yvette's condition. What type of treatment would you recommend if you followed the cognitive model of abnormal behavior? If you followed the psychoanalytic model?

4)   Considering the impact on her life the numbness could have, Yvette seems relatively unconcerned about her condition. In what way is her calmness not surprising?

63. Abnormal Behavior - Mood Disorders

Joanne is a college sophomore. Growing up in a middle-class suburban environment, the only daughter of second-generation Mexican-American parents, her life has been a happy one. However, when she moved away from home to attend college in the East, Joanne began to experience periods of extreme sadness. She missed her family and worried about having to make new friends.

Although Joanne's "bad days", as she called them, were infrequent during her first year at college, returning for her second was even more difficult. In her first year, her sadness over leaving home was tempered by the excitement of living in a new place. Now that the newness was wearing off, Joanne's bad days were becoming more common. Fortunately, Joanne's mother began to notice her daughter's symptoms, having gone through the same kind of thing after giving birth. She convinced Joanne to speak with a campus counselor.

1) How would the most recent revision of the DSM diagnose Joanne's condition? How does this condition differ from bipolar disorder?

2) The most widely used treatment for Joanne's condition is through drug therapy. Does this imply that the root of her problem is biological? In your answer distinguish between a disease and its symptoms. (Consider aspirin as an analogy.)

3)   How can the concept of learned helplessness explain why some people become depressed? What evidence suggests a cognitive explanation of depression may be correct?

4)   As a woman, Joanne's chances of experiencing depression are relatively greater. How is this differential vulnerability explained by the cognitive and medical models?

64. Abnormal Behavior - Dissociative Disorders

In 1926, The celebrated English author Agatha Christie disappeared in what was suspected by many to be a kidnapping, or murder. Following a nationwide search, she was discovered staying at a spa in northern England under an assumed name. Many suspected the whole affair had been a publicity stunt, and Dame Agatha's only public explanation was that she could not remember how she came to be where she was.

Today, we may be in a better position to understand what really happened to Ms. Christie. A few months before her disappearance, her mother passed away. When her husband refused to involve himself in the matter, she was forced to handle the complicated settling of affairs on her own. If these events weren't difficult enough, Agatha was in for a greater shock. Her husband of more than 20 years revealed that he had been having an affair and was leaving her. It was shortly after this revelation that Agatha disappeared.

1) Do the events that preceded Agatha Christie's disappearance make her story about memory loss seem plausible? Why or why not?

2) Assuming that her explanation is correct, how would the DSM diagnose her condition? How does psychogenic amnesia differ from psychogenic fugue? Of the two, which is more common?

3) How might each of the following models of abnormal behavior explain Agatha's case: psychoanalytic, medical, socio-cultural? Which explanation do you prefer? Defend your answer.

4) When asked about how she got to be where she was, Agatha claimed not to remember. Is it common for sufferers of this disorder to have no memory of such periods?

5) The name under which Agatha registered at the spa was that of her husband's mistress. Is it usual for sufferers of this disorder to have memories of the events that triggered their episode?

65. Treating Abnormal Behavior - Psychodynamic Approaches

Jody has suffered from generalized anxiety disorder for several years. Although he is young, intelligent, and articulate, social settings have always made him uncomfortable. Six months ago, he decided to get professional help, and has since been meeting with a therapist twice a week.

At first, he was uncomfortable talking about personal issues with a relative stranger, but that quickly passed. Jody's relationship with his therapist is today as close as with any friend he has ever had. During their sessions, he talks about important events in his life and she just listens. Then she'll ask him about recent dreams he has had and they try to decode their meaning. For example, Jody frequently dreams of flying, and he now realizes that this represents his desire to be financially independent. Jody values these times together very much and feels that he has made great progress in the time that he has been in therapy.

1) Of what orientation is Jody's therapist? How would you classify the approach that she is using to treat his anxiety?

2) What is the manifest content of Jody's dream described in this story? What is the latent content of the dream?

3)   Is it unusual for patients to feel as close to their therapists as Jody does? How can this closeness be beneficial to a therapeutic relationship? In what way can this closeness be harmful?

4)   Jody feels that his therapy has been a success. What evidence suggests that this therapy will indeed be successful? Consider both his condition and his personality.

5)   How would Jody's therapist describe the cause of his problem. How does the type of therapy described in this story resolve the roots of his anxiety? What assumptions about generalized anxiety disorder is she making?

66. Treating Abnormal Behavior - Cognitive and Behavioral Approaches

Shortly after her youngest daughter Tammy moved away to college, Barbara began to experience long periods of loneliness and depression. "It's only natural," she told herself, "it will go away."

But over the next few months her bouts of depressions only became more frequent and more severe. That was when she decided to seek counseling.

At first, her therapist wanted to prescribe an anti-depressant drug. But Barbara was uncomfortable with the idea of taking drugs. They therefore decided to take a different approach and was instructed to keep a diary of the times that she felt the most depressed. From this diary, she and her therapist discovered that she was most depressed on Saturday and Sunday mornings. When Barbara thought about why this should be so, she realized that it was during this time that she and Tammy had spent most of their quality time in recent years. Now these mornings only reminded her that she wasn't needed anymore and that her life was meaningless.

1) What type of therapist is Barbara seeing? What type of degree does the therapist have? Explain your answer.

2) What approach has her therapist decided to take with Barbara? Is she undergoing psychotherapy? What psychologist is most closely associated with this type of therapy?

3)   Now that they have discovered why weekend mornings are so difficult for Barbara, what is the next step? How will her therapist help her overcome her weekend episodes of depressions?

4)   What is the eclectic approach to therapy? Is there any evidence that Barbara's therapist uses such an approach?

67. Treating Abnormal Behavior - Humanistic and Group Therapy

Now in his fourth year of graduate school in clinical psychology, Michael has been thinking about what area of the profession he will pursue after graduation. He has developed a strong background in cognitive and behavioral approaches, in psychodynamic approaches, and also in humanistic approaches. However, when he begins his own practice, Michael wants to focus on only one of these approaches.

One issue that concerns Michael is how directive he could be as a therapist. Admittedly he is not a very forceful person and would be more comfortable as a more non-directive therapist. A second concern is whether he should chose a long-term or shorter-term style of therapy. Although the idea of the steady, long-term client is appealing, Michael is afraid he might tire of seeing the same patients after a while. For this reason, he would prefer a therapeutic approach that could meet its objectives quickly.

1)   On the basis of Michael's desire to practice a short-termed, nondirective style of therapy, which of the four approaches with which he is familiar should he chose, and why?

2)   Michael believes that people's behavior is heavily influenced by past experiences. For this reason he prefers a therapy that focuses on early experiences and less on the here and now. Considering this, which style of therapy should he chose? Defend you answer.

3)   One of the areas with which Michael is interested in working is phobias. On the basis of your answer to question #1, Is it likely that Michael will be able to help people with simple phobias? If so, how? If not, why?

4)   Some therapeutic approaches focus on changing the thoughts, or cognitions, of clients while others focus on changing concrete behaviors. On the basis of you answer to question #1, where will Michael's approach fall on this dimension?

5)   Compared with other types of therapies, how effective is the type chosen by Michael (question #1)? What difficulties make it hard to answer this question?

68. Treating Abnormal Behavior - Comparing Psychotherapeutic Approaches

Mary has been smoking cigarettes since she was 15. Now, at age 30, she would like to quit. After several attempts to quit on her own failed, she decided to get help and enrolled in a therapy group for people trying to kick an addictive habit. Most people in the group are trying to stop drinking, a few others smoking, and some harder drugs.

In her weekly meetings with the group, people take turns sharing experiences related to their addiction. However, Mary usually doesn't talk very much, feeling that other group members, who are having more difficulty than she, should get more of the group's attention. Never the less, she enjoys going. The therapist is very warm and seems genuinely to care about each member of the group. He tells them people are responsible for their own behavior and that their addictions are caused by insecurities. By learning to trust themselves, the members are becoming more self-reliant and less dependent on smoking, drugs, and alcohol.

1)   What approach is Mary's therapist taking? What are some of the specific types of therapies within this general approach? How do they differ from one another?

2)   In what ways might group therapy be an especially good method for treating addictive behaviors? Are there any drawbacks to this method? Will these drawbacks affect all group members equally?

3)   Describe the concept of unconditional positive regard. Is there any evidence that Mary's therapist is using this concept in his treatment?

4)   An important part of their therapy sessions every week is in acting out the anger that has built up over the week by hitting pillows. This is characteristic of what type of therapy? What is the rationale for this type of acting out?

69. Attitudes and Social Cognition - Attitudes and Persuasion

After receiving her bachelor's degree in psychology last year, Hillary was able to find employment in a small advertising firm in Boston. One of her first assignments was to come up with an idea for a television ad campaign for Spiffy, a new brand of fabric detergent. Although Spiffy is a new product, it does not possess any special quality that separates it from competing brands. The makers of Spiffy plan to price their product so that it is competitive with, but not substantially cheaper than, other major brands. Taking all of this into account, Hillary decides to design her campaign around a slogan that is catchy but relatively weak. Two of her ideas were: "There's clean, and then there's Spiffy", or "When something is really clean, you call it Spiffy."

1) Which "route" to persuasion is Hillary attempting to use? What are the liabilities of using such an approach?

2) Will source factors or message characteristics be more important in Hillary's ad?

3)   Unfortunately, the amount of money that Spiffy is willing to spend on this campaign is limited. Because of the limited budget, Hilary decides to use an attractive but unknown model in her commercial. What learning principle is she trying to utilize? Is her decision a good one? Why or why not?

4)   After further thought, Hilary changes her mind and decides to include strong statements about why Spiffy is superior to competing products. In addition, she is considering using a well known spokesperson to deliver these arguments. Would changing spokespersons be a good idea? Defend your answer.

5)   Is there any reason to believe that one of the two tentative slogans would work better than the other? Defend your answer.

70. Attitudes and Social Cognition - Attitudes and Behavior

Sean, a sophomore biology major at a large Midwestern college, is at home in New York for the summer. Hoping to put aside some money for the fall, he found a part-time work doing odd jobs at the Bronx Zoo. In general he enjoys his work and has learned much about the many different species under his care. Although Sean has gotten used to being around some of the larger (and potentially dangerous) animals, he is still not comfortable being around the snakes in the reptile exhibit. He tells himself again and again that snakes are harmless, but it doesn't seem to work. After a month, going into the reptile exhibit is as difficult as it was on his first day of work.

1)   How would you respond to the question "What is Sean's attitude towards snakes?" Can the ABC model of attitudes account for Sean's mixed feelings about snakes?

2)   Is Sean's behavior likely to be consistent with his cognitions or his affect about snakes?

3)   According to cognitive dissonance theory, how might Sean reduce his mixed feelings about snakes?

4)   Imagine that Sean's supervisor offers him $50 more a week if he agrees to assume responsibility for feeding the reptiles every morning. How might Sean's acceptance of this offer affect his attitude towards snakes? If Sean refused this offer, how might that affect his attitude? How would your answer to these questions change if Sean was offered just $2 extra a week instead of $50?

5)   Sean decides to accept responsibility for feeding the reptiles at no increase in pay because he thinks that this will help him overcome his fear. What does self-perception theory predict about the success of this attempt? Does this prediction differ from that made by cognitive dissonance theory? If so, how?

71. Attitudes and Social Cognition - Understanding Others and Stereotypes

Jared, an African-American student at a private liberal arts college, is enrolled in a large introductory psychology course taught by Dr. Frohlich. When the last of four "critical thinking" papers were handed back, Jared was surprised and disappointed to find that he had received a B-. He had spent a fair amount of time and effort preparing this paper. After re-reading the paper and the comments made by the teaching assistant who graded the paper, Jared still believed that the paper deserved an A. A friend who had taken the class before encouraged him to see his professor, explaining that Dr. Frohlich was basically a warm and approachable person.

Jared met with his professor and began to explain why he believed that he deserved a higher grade. Almost immediately, Dr. Frohlich interrupted him and agreed to raise the grade to an A.

1) How might Jared's belief in Dr. Frohlich warm character have affected this particular interaction? Would Jared's impression of the interaction have been different had he expected Dr. Frohlich to be a cold person? Defend your answer.

2) Dan, the teaching assistant who originally graded Jared's paper, holds no negative stereotypes of African-Americans. Is it still possible that his grading of Jared's paper was discriminatory? Why or why not.

3)   Why might Jared feel unsatisfied after having his grade raised? What negative consequences might result from his experience with Dr. Frohlich?

4)   Assume that Dr. Frohlich believes that as a group, African-Americans are less prepared for college-level work than are Anglo-Americans. Is it likely that interaction with well-prepared students such as Jared would change this negative belief?

72. Attitudes and Cognition - Attributions I

Laura would have been ready for her date on time, but Kevin arrived early. The sound of the doorbell set of the usual series of sharp barks from her Yorkshire terrier, Dillo (short for Armadillo). After calming Dillo down, Laura went to get her jacket from her bedroom, but the jacket was not were she remembered putting it. This annoyance at not being able to find her jacket was heightened by a return of Dillo's yip-barks in the other room. With exaggerated steps, Laura stamped back into the living room and began yelling for Dillo to be quiet. To this day, Laura is not sure whether the scene she walked in on was more funny or sad. Upon returning to the living area, Laura was startled to find Kevin holding Dillo - and biting him on the leg!

1)   According to Kelly's attributional model, what questions would be running through Laura's mind?

2)   Suppose that Laura recalls that Kevin has done this before. According to Kelly's model, would this suggest a dispositional cause or a situational cause of Kevin's behavior? Do you agree?

3)   How might the Pollyanna effect influence Laura's attributions in this situation? Is the Halo effect likely to factor into her decision?

4)   According to the fundamental attribution bias, is Laura likely to blame Kevin for this ugly incident? What explanations for the incident is Kevin likely to give?

5)   Imagine that this is Laura's first date with Kevin and that she just purchased Dillo that afternoon. What prediction would Kelly's model make about her attributions for this event? Do you view this prediction as a weakness in Kelly's model?

In addition to taking thirteen hours of courses this semester, Tom is holding down a part-time job delivering pizza's on weekends and occasionally on weekday evenings. One recent Sunday evening, Tom arrived home after an exhausting eight hours at work. Walking past the phone, he noticed the light on his answering machine was blinking indicating that there were three messages waiting to be heard. Being very tired and not feeling like talking to anyone, Tom decided to listen to the messages but not bother with them tonight unless they were important. The third message was from Jeff, a guy in his calculus class that he only casually knew. Jeff was apparently having difficulty with an assignment that was due in the morning and was hoping that he could discuss it tonight. After pouring and quickly drinking a glass a water, Tom lethargically undressed and fell quickly asleep on his bed, without returning his calls.

1)   Based on your knowledge of attribution theory, what reasons would Tom give for his not returning Jeff's call? What reasons would Jeff postulate for Tom's behavior?

2)   According to self-perception theory, how might this event affect Tom's friendship with Jeff?

3)   Actually, Tom himself has not yet completed the assignment. Although calculus assignments usually require considerable time and effort, Tom believes that he'll be able to finish it quickly in the morning. Is such overconfidence a sign of poor or good psychological health?

4)   Imagine that Tom is a Japanese exchange student. How might this cultural difference have contributed to his decision not to return Jeff's call?

5)   In what way is self-perception theory in conflict with attribution theory in predicting how Tom would explain his own behavior? Can both theories be correct?

Critical Thinking: General Principles and Case Studies

74. Social Influences and Interactions - Social Influences

Joanne is a manager at a large grocery store chain. Recently she instituted a program to increase the productivity of the cash register workers. Establishing a base rate, she decided that for the next two weeks workers who perform at a rate that is at least 5% higher than base rate (a small request) will receive a weekly bonus of $20. However, in the third week, Joanne plans to offer the bonus only to those workers who increase their productivity by 10% (a medium request).

But Joanne's plan is not finished after three weeks. In the fourth week, she will tell her workers that only those who increase productivity by 15% (a large request) will receive a bonus. Expecting workers to complain about this higher standard, Joanne's final move will be to agree to lower the productivity bonus requirement back to 10% above base rate levels.

1)   Explain how Joanne has taken advantage of the "foot-in-the-door" to increase her workers' productivity. In which week will the benefits of this technique pay off?

2)   What other closely related technique does Joanne's plan utilize? In which week will the benefits of this second technique pay off?

3)   Imagine that Joanne's workers become upset by the bonus requirement being raised to 15%. Sensing that more subtle persuasion may be needed, she lies and says that she will try to get upper management to lower to requirement to 8% in week four, knowing full well that in fact, the requirement will be 10% as planned. Is this lie likely to be effective? Why or why not?

4)   Are the techniques utilized by Joanne conformity techniques, compliance techniques, or obedience techniques? Suggest perfusion methods that use the type(s) of techniques Joanne did not.

75. Social Influences and Interactions - Liking and Loving: Interpersonal Attraction

Tracy and Steve got married this summer. At the wedding, Tracy's father recalled aloud how often he had heard her say that a good man was hard to find, that the combination of qualities she was looking for just didn't seem to exist. But then came Steve.

It was hardly love at first sight for Tracy. She and two friends were moving out of the dorms and were looking for a fourth person to fill a four bedroom house they had rented near campus. When Steve showed up to apply for the room, Tracy hesitantly conceded that he would be an acceptable roommate. By the end of their first semester Steve and Tracy were happily dating, and two years later were married.

1)   Tracy's father thought that it was ironic that, after looking everywhere for a perfect match, she meet her future husband right in her own home. Would social psychologists find this so ironic? Why or why not?

2)   When asked why she decided to marry Steve, Tracy said she just fell in love with the things he did: the way he sang in the shower, his way of styling his hair, even his unique walk, the result of an old knee injury. Although she thought these qualities were slightly odd at first, now she couldn't imagine loving someone without them. What psychological phenomenon is operating here?

3)   Steve never heard that Tracy found him a barely acceptable roommate upon their first meeting until after they had been dating for nearly a year. If this had been revealed earlier, how might it have affected their relationship?

4)   When Tracy moved, she moved in with her current roommate and a friend of theirs who lived next door. Is her choice of housemates a coincidence, or are some psychological factors at work here?

5)   According to Steve, his decision to date Tracy had less to do with how attractive she was, and more to do with her personality. Tracy just seemed like a really good person. Assuming that Steve is correct about his reasons, is it possible that her physical attractiveness still impacted his decision? Explain your answer.

Tony meet Cassy during band camp. Every year, members of the marching band are required to return to campus two weeks early to attend band camp and to prepare for the first football game, which is also their first performance of the year. Both Tony and Cassy were freshman that year, and both were involved in dating relationships that had extended past their senior year of high school. However, they became fast friends.

A year later, both returned to band camp unattached. Although neither of them had thought about dating each other the previous year, they now both experienced pangs of attraction for one another. Hesitant at first that dating might result in damaging a valued friendship, they decided to give it a chance. They have been going out for over a year now.

1)   Band camp can be a very stressful experience. How might this have affected the attraction that Cassy and Tony felt for one another?

2)   The first year Cassy and Tony knew one another, they told their friends that they liked each other very much. A year later, they told their friends that they loved each other. According to the dominant school of thought in love research, what had changed about their feelings for one another? Did their feelings change qualitatively or quantitatively?

3)   According to Robert Sternberg's triangle theory of love, what component of love characterized the liking that friends feel for one another? When Cassy and Tony decided to commit themselves to a relationship, what component was added? What type of love did this create?

4)   Consider a statement that Tony made about Cassy to a close friend. "Cassy," he said, "has her share of faults. But overall they are pretty small compared to her strengths." Is this comment characteristic of a relationship that is just beginning, is mature and successful, or one that is mature and beginning to deteriorate?

77. Social Influences and Interactions - Aggression

Judy is considering giving up her subscription to the newspaper. All of the violence and tragedy in the world, and even in her own community, is getting to be too depressing. For example, in today's addition there is a front page article about terrorists in Gilder detonating a car bomb near a night club frequented by military personal. The terrorists claim that the bombing is in response to a recent attack on their headquarters made by the Gilder military, whose personnel were the targets of the car bomb.

Closer to home, the city council has cut funds to the animal shelter in an effort reduce a projected multi-million dollar budget deficit. As a result the shelter will no longer hold for adoption dogs and cats that are more than a year old. Older animals, which are not adopted as quickly, will be destroyed after being held one day. Also slated for cutting is the amount of support provided to the city's charity hospital, which will be forced to reduce it's number of beds by 20%.

1)   Which of the following acts do you feel constitute aggression: the detonation of the car bomb, the attack on terrorist headquarters, the shelter destroying stray animals, the city council's reducing aid to the animal shelter and to the charity hospital, the hospital for turning away those who need help when no beds are available?

2)   Some psychologists define aggression as "intentionally hurting another person." According to this definition, which of the five acts described would constitute "aggression?" Does the action of the terrorists and the Gilder military differ with respect to being classified as aggression or non-aggression?

3)   Is there a difference doing something in order to hurt someone, and doing something that you know will hurt someone but you do it anyway? What does this imply about the city's cutting the budget of programs they know will result in hurting people in need of help.

4)   According to instinct theories of aggression, why are humans aggressive? If psychologists wanted to reduce the amount of violence in their community, what type of programs would instinct theory suggest they implement?

5)   How do frustration-aggression theorists explain the situation that is going on Gilder. What types of programs would psychologists from this school of thought implement in order to reduce the hostility in this country.

78. Social Influences and Interactions - Prosocial Behavior

The doctors told Mr. Crepeau that he was a lucky man because for many people the first heart attack is their last. However, it's was a little hard for him to feel lucky just now. Then again, he had to admit that things could have been much worse if it hadn't been for the assistance of two legal secretaries.

John Crepeau had been coming home from work much later than usual when began to feel unusual sensations. When his arms began to grow numb and he felt light headed and dizzy, John asked aloud if someone could help him. Taken aback, no one on the commuter train knew what to do. Becoming more forceful, John pointed to a woman nearby and said, "You! Can you help me? I think I'm having a heart attack." She immediately came over to help. Recognizing more help was needed, a second person ran to tell the conductor while a third began looking for a doctor or nurse on neighboring cars.

1)   At first, no one knew how to react to John's request for aid. What psychological phenomenon may have prevented these bystanders from taking action? How did John's second request overcome this obstacle?

2)   Although it was difficult to get the first person to help him, she was quickly followed by two others. How did the first helper's behavior influence that of the second and third helpers.

3)   To those who viewed John's heart attack, two questions must have gone through their mind: Does this man need help, and if so, should I be the one to help. What psychological phenomena make these two questions difficult for the bystanders to answer?

4)   According to learning theorists, would those who witnessed John's heart attack, but did not help, be likely to give help if they were in this type of situation again? What would moral reasoning theorists, such as Kohlberg, say about these inactive bystanders and the likelihood that they would help in other similar situations?

79. Consumer and Industrial Psychology - Consumer Psychology I

Teressa was in the market for a notebook computer. Rather than paying top dollar at a local dealer, she reasoned that she could save money by looking through a mail order catalogue. While reading an issue of "Direct Buy Computers", Teressa's attention was grabbed by a full color insert that showed a woman dressed in an athletic outfit sitting in a sunny meadow in front of her mountain bike. Under this beautiful photo was the slogan, "Zenix computers will set you free."

However, on the very next page a more direct add also drew her attention. "Uno computers," explained this add, "outperform the competition, and they do it for less money."

Indeed, the Uno models ran about $100 less than Zenix. After weighing her options, Teressa made a decision: she would get an Uno system.

1) Advertisers and psychologists can distinguish between hard-sell tactics and soft-sell tactics. Which of these two approaches was taken by the advertisers of Zenix computers? By Uno computers?

2) How does the concept of "self-monitoring" affect the persuasiveness of hard- and soft-sell tactics? Would you say that Teressa was high or low in this characteristic?

3)   The makers of Zenix computers had considered running an advertisement that was similar to Uno's, but their research in high schools showed a consistent preference for the ad that Teressa saw in her magazine. What might have gone wrong?

4)   The next day, when deciding which type of spaghetti sauce to purchase at the grocery store, Teressa was persuaded by an image based add and not a reason based add. Why might she have been persuaded by different types of advertising appeals on these two occasions?

80. Consumer and Industrial Psychology - Consumer Psychology II

Mr. McKean was opening his mail when he came across an ad for the new line of Johnny-Lawn lawn mowers caught his attention. It just so happened that he was in the market for a new mower. Although he owned several other J-L products, he had never owed one of their mowers. Mr. McKean decided to go to the library to look through past issues of <u>Consumer Reports</u> and see if they had tested these mowers. Surprisingly, it turned out that Johnny-Lawn had received one of the lowest ratings.

He then decided to phone a friend from work, who he knew had recently purchased a J-L mower. According to her, she was very happy with her decision; it started easily, ran smoothly, and had an easy to remove grass bagging system. Mr. McKean was convinced.

1) Before making his purchase decision, Mr. McKean consulted three different types of advice. What were they? What important type of advice did he fail to seek out?

2) Accepting the advice of his co-worker may have been a mistake. What psychological phenomenon may have erroneously inflated her personal attitude towards J-L mowers? What is the danger in such anecdotal evidence?

3)   Categorize Mr. McKean's reasons for purchasing a J-L mower according to whether they were product attributes or brand beliefs.

4)   How might the advertisers of J-L mowers use micromarketing to identify which homes to mail their advertisement? How might psychographic techniques helped them in this task?

81. Consumer and Industrial Psychology - Industrial/Organizational Psychology: Workers

Professor Olson teaches an introductory level biology class at a large university. In the past years her class has become considerably larger, while the average student grade has dropped. In order to reverse this trend in grades, Dr. Olson has decided to incorporate motivation techniques from industrial psychology into her fall classes.

One technique that she has decided to adapt is to have students set specific goals the week before every exam. Another technique is to allow students to decide for themselves the format of the exams. Finally, Dr. Olson plans to call five students at random every evening and check on their progress in preparing for the next exam. She hopes that instituting these changes will improve her students' grades.

1) Which of the three theories of motivation is Dr. Olson using by asking students to set specific goals for themselves: Need theory, cognitive theory, or reinforcement theory? Can you devise a technique that uses one of the other two theories?

2) Would allowing students to choose for themselves the format of their exams improve their satisfaction in taking Dr. Olson's class? Would it improve their motivation to do well in her class? Defend your answers.

3) Which model of management is Dr. Olson using by closely monitoring her students' progress? Which model of management is she using by allowing students to choose their own test format?

4) Evaluate the three techniques that Dr. Olson plans to institute to raise her students grades? Which do you think will be the most helpful? Which will be the least helpful?

5) In general, how would you describe the job of being a student in terms of job clarity? In terms of role-conflict? Provide example to back up your answers.

Critical Thinking: General Principles and Case Studies

82. Consumer and Industrial Psychology - Industrial/Organizational Psychology: Organizations

Peter Johnson has a difficult job. As the manager of a fast food restaurant, Pete has to balance the needs of his employees with the demands of his employer. Unfortunately, his employees are largely unconcerned with the success of the company, and his employer is largely unconcerned with employee satisfaction.

Peter has long recognized that the longer a person is employed with the restaurant, the better they are as a worker. However, most people he hires quit after a few months. In order to reduce the problem of turnover, Peter has decided to have company parties twice a year. He hopes this will give employees a chance to get to know one other better. Perhaps it would be harder to quit a job at which one had many friends. Additionally, Peter plans to train workers to do more than one job at the restaurant, to increase their awareness of "the big picture."

1) What aspects of Peter's plan may improve employee satisfaction? Will this satisfaction directly improve their value as an employee? Will it directly improve their value as an employee?

2) How satisfied do you think Peter feels in his job? Be sure to address both role conflict and the centralization of decision making.

3)   Can you identify any elements of Japanese management style in Peter's intended changes? What (other) Japanese management techniques might Peter be able to apply?

4)   How does Peter's plan make use of need theories of motivation? How might he have made use of cognitive theories of motivation? Of reinforcement theories?

83. Consumer and Industrial Psychology - Industrial/Organizational Psychology: Decision Making

Jen, the residence director of a co-ed dormitory, is getting ready for the first meeting of the semester with her RA staff. Many issues will need to be addressed and Jen is making a mental list of them in preparation. For example, should decision regarding punishments for hall infractions be made on the spot by individual RAs or groups of RAs in weekly meetings? Then there is the decision to be made regarding how to spend the projected $400 budget surplus. Third, a list of objectives for the RA staff be made. Jen is personally generating this list and will share them at tonight's meeting. Finally, she plans to take the first few minutes of the meeting by having her staff brainstorm the problem of parking. It appears there are not enough parking spots for all of the RAs who request them, and Jen is not sure what to do about it.

1) Consider the issue of whether individual RAs or groups should decide the fate of rule violators in the dorm. What are the advantages and disadvantages of each method? Which would you choose?

2) Do you agree or disagree with Jen's decision to personally generate the list of staff objectives? What is the best method for generating such a list?

3)   Jen would like to hear as many ideas about how to solve the parking situation as possible. Is brainstorming the best way to do this? Why or why not?

4)   How should Jen and her staff go about deciding how to spend the budget surplus? Specify the format (group versus individual) that she should use to generate ideas, evaluate those ideas, and eventually choose from among them.

5)   During the meeting, someone proposed a new way of dealing with conflicts in the dorm. Perhaps Jen should personally make a decision about how to discipline rule infractions and then direct RAs to carry out her decision. Evaluate this idea in terms of group decision dynamics.

References

Asch, S. E. (1951). Effects of group pressure upon the modification and distortion of judgments. In H. Guertzkow (Ed.), <u>Groups, leadership, and men.</u> Pittsburgh: Carnegie Press.

Bell, A., Weinberg, M., & Hammersmith, S. (1981). <u>Sexual preference: Its development in men and women.</u> Bloomington: Indiana University Press.

Bransford, J.D., & Stein, B.S. (1984). <u>The ideal problem solver: A guide for improving thinking, learning and creativity</u>. New York: W.H. Freeman and Company.

Brookfield, S.D. (1987). <u>Developing critical thinkers.</u> San Francisco: Jossey-Bass.

Costa, R.M. (1982, March 6). Latin and Greek are good for you. <u>The New York Times,</u> p.23.

D'Andrade, R. (1982). Paper presented at the Symposium on the Ecology of Cognition: Biological, Cultural, and Historical Perspectives, Greensboro, NC.

D'Angelo, E. (1971). <u>The teaching of critical thinking.</u> Amsterdam: B.R. Gruner.

Darley, J.M., & Latané, B. (1968). Bystanders intervention in emergencies: Diffusion of responsibility. <u>Journal of Personality and Social Psychology, 8,</u> 377-383.

Duncker, K. (1945). <u>On problem solving</u> (L.S. Lees, Trans.) <u>Psychological Monographs, 58.</u>

Eastman, N.J. (1957). <u>Expectant motherhood</u> (3rd revised E.). Boston: Little, Brown   and Company.

Fiske, S.T., & Taylor, S.E. (1984). <u>Social cognition</u>. Reading, MA: Addison-Wesley.

Halpern, D.F. (1984). <u>Thought and knowledge: An introduction to critical thinking</u>. Hillsdale, NJ: Erlbaum.

Hooker, E. (1957). The adjustment of the male overt homosexual. <u>Journal of Projective Techniques, 21,</u> 18-31.

Hooker, E. (1968). Homosexuality. In <u>International Encyclopedia of Social Sciences.</u> New York: MacMillan.

James, W. (1899). Talks to teachers on psychology; and to students on some of life's ideals. New York: Holt.

Janoff-Bulman, R. (1989). Assumptive worlds and the stress of traumatic events: Application of the schema construct. Social Cognition, special issue: "Social Cognition and Stress."

Latané, B., & Darley, J.M. (1976). Help in a crisis: Bystander response to an emergency. In J.W. Thibaut, J.T. Spence, and R.C. Carson (Eds.), Contemporary topics in social psychology. Morristown, N.J.: General Learning Press.

Lehman, D.R., Lempert, R.O., & Nisbett, R.E. (1988). The effects of graduate training on reasoning. American Psychologist, 43, 431-442.

Miller, S.I., & Schoenfeld, L. (1973). Grief in the Navajo: Psychodynamics and culture. International Journal of Social Psychiatry, 19, 187-911.

Nisbett, R.E., Fong. G.T., Lehman, D.R., & Cheng, P.W. (1987). Teaching reasoning. Science, 238, 625-631.

Osborn, A.F. (1963). Applied imagination: Principles and procedures of creative problem solving (3rd Revised Ed.). New York: Scribner's.

Peirce, C.S. (1960). In C. Hartshorne and P. Weiss (Eds.), Collected Papers: Vol. 5: Pragmatism and pragmaticism, 2nd ed. Cambridge: Harvard University Press.

Pollock, G. (1972). On mourning and anniversaries: The relationship of culturally constituted defense systems to intra-psychic adaptive processes. Israeli Annals of Psychiatry, 10, 9-40.

Rosenblatt, P.C., Walsh, R.P., & Jackson, D.A. (1976). Grief and mourning in cross-cultural perspective. New Haven: Yale: HRAF.

Saghir, M., & Robins, E. (1971). Male and female homosexuality: Natural history. Comprehensive Psychiatry, 11, 503-510.

Saghir, M., & Robins, E. (1973). Male and female homosexuality: A comprehensive investigation. Baltimore: Williams & Wilkins.

Sternberg, R.J., & Caruso, D. (1985). Practical modes of knowing. IN E. Eisner (Ed.), Learning the ways of knowing. Chicago: University of Chicago Press.

Strauss, J.S., & Carpenter, W.T., Jr. (1981). Schizophrenia. New York: Plenum.

Thorndike. E.L. (1906). Principles of teaching. New York: A.G. Seiler.

Thorndike, E.L. (1913). <u>The psychology of learning</u>. New York: Mason-Henry.

Wason, P.C. (1966). Reasoning. In B.M. Foss (Ed.), <u>New horizons in psychology</u>.
Harmondsworth, England: Penguin.

Winter, D.G. (1984). Reconstructing introductory psychology. In K.I. Spear (Ed.),
<u>New directions for teaching and learning, no. 20</u> (pp. 77 - 88).
San Francisco: Jossey-Bass.